"*Occupy* is another vital contribution from Chomsky to the literature of defiance and protest, and a red-hot rallying call to forge a better, more egalitarian future."

—Don Hazen, *AlterNet*

"For decades, Chomsky has been marginalized for his insightful, levelheaded, and accurate observations about how our society functions. In *Occupy*, Chomsky . . . sets the record straight. And he's got an answer for everything. 'It's necessary,' Chomsky warns, 'to get out into the country and get people to understand what this is about, and what they can do about it, and what the consequences are of not doing anything about it.' One can only cringe at the thought of what will happen if we continue to ignore the wisdom of Noam Chomsky. He gives a clue in *Occupy*. . . ."

—*The Coffin Factory: The Magazine for People Who Love Books*

"Chomsky advocates intelligent activism by those who see the divorce between public policy and public opinion. He is both optimistic and realistic towards this 'first major public response to 30 years of class war.'"

—*Irish Times*

"*Occupy* is at once a vivid portrait of the now-global movement and a practical guide to intelligent activism, infused with Chomsky's signature meditations on everything from how the wealthiest 1% came to steer society, to what a healthy democracy would look like, to how we can separate money from politics. Alongside Chomsky's words are some of the most moving and provocative photographs from the Occupy movement."

—Maria Popova, *Brain Pickings*

"Having spent so much time thinking about and engaging with social movements, Chomsky is both optimistic about the energy of Occupy and realistic about the challenges it faces. He appreciates the 'just do it' ethos and embraces its radical approach to participatory democracy . . . What makes Chomsky's perspective so interesting, aside from the wealth of his political experience, is the range of his interests. He draws from examples around the world to demonstrate his points. . . . It's a big agenda that Occupy has identified, nothing less than a complete renewal of U.S. society and the U.S. role in the world. Chomsky sees not only the radical agenda but also the radical practice of the Occupiers. 'Part of what functioning, free communities like the Occupy communities can be working for and spreading to others is just a different way of living, which is not based on maximizing consumer goods, but on maximizing values that are important for life,' he concludes in this valuable set of remarks and interviews."

—John Feffer, *Foreign Policy in Focus*, Pick Review

OCCUPY

NOAM CHOMSKY

2ND EDITION

Occupied Media Pamphlet Series | Zuccotti Park Press

WESTFIELD, NEW JERSEY

Cover design by R. Black

Special thanks to Eliot Katz for proofreading.

This publication is a joint project of Zuccotti Park Press, Adelante Alliance and Essential Information.

ISBN: 978-1-884519-25-3

Library of Congress Control Number: 2013937442

Printed in the United States of America

9 8 7 6 5 4 3 2 1

Zuccotti Park Press
PO Box 2726, Westfield, NJ 07090
occupy@adelantealliance.org
www.zuccottiparkpress.com

CONTENTS

Art and Photography

Cover art
R. Black

Inside cover
Brooklyn Bridge
Copyright © 2011 Stanley Rogouski

Page 8
Brooklyn Bridge, October 1, 2011
Copyright © 2011 Alex Fradkin

Pages 20–21
Occupy
Copyright © 2011 Alex Fradkin

Page 22
Chomsky addresses Occupy Boston, October 22, 2011
Copyright © 2011 Scott Eisen

Page 52
Zuccotti Park
Copyright © 2011 Stanley Rogouski

Page 68
Zuccotti Park
Copyright © 2011 Alex Fradkin

Page 88
Zuccotti Park
Copyright © 2011 Stanley Rogouski

Pages 110–111
Brooklyn Bridge, October 1, 2011
Copyright © 2011 Alex Fradkin

Page 112
Foley Square
Copyright © 2011 Alex Fradkin

Page 124
Zuccotti Park
Copyright © 2011 Stanley Rogouski

Page 136
Brooklyn Bridge, October 1, 2011
Copyright © 2011 Alex Fradkin

Dedicated to the 7,762 people who have been arrested at movement actions to date, from the first 80 arrested marching in New York City on September 24, 2011, to the two people arrested on June 15, 2013 when San Francisco Police raided the "Liberate the Land" encampment outside the former site of Hayes Valley farm, which protesters had occupied for weeks.*

* "Two protesters arrested outside former Hayes Valley farm site," ABC News KGO-TV San Francisco, June 15 2013. http://abclocal.go.com/kgo/story?section=news/local/san_francisco&id=9140428

EDITOR'S NOTE

"Occupy," says Noam Chomsky, "is the first major public response to thirty years of class war," a people-powered movement that began in New York City on September 17, 2011, and rapidly spread to thousands of locations worldwide. Although those in the movement have been subject to widespread surveillance, infiltration, mass arrests and illegal operations reminiscent of the COINTELPRO era, the international networks forged during Occupy continue to develop projects and protests as an open-ended expression of its vision of democracy-centered civil society.

In the first edition of *Occupy*, Chomsky pointed out that one of the movement's greatest successes was to put the inequalities of everyday life on the national agenda, influencing reporting, public awareness and language itself. Referencing a January 2012 Pew Research Center report on public perceptions of class conflict within the United States, Chomsky notes that inequalities in the country "have risen to historically unprecedented heights." The Pew study found that about two-thirds of the U.S. population became aware that there are "very strong" or "strong" conflicts between the rich and the poor—an increase of 19 percentage points since 2009.[*]

Months of widespread protest and mobilization changed the national political conversation, and it is important to acknowledge all the people who camped out, marched or went to jail to help make it happen. While not a single banker has been arrested for committing the crimes of economic mass destruction that have devastated the nation, as of July 2013, more than 7,760 people in 122 U.S. cities have been arrested while engaging in movement-related activity. As Occupy became a national then global phenomenon, there was a clear increase in coverage of issues relating to income disparity, as well as increased use of the movement's language in official political discourse. Getting politicians and the press to sound like social justice advocates has never been one the movement's goals, but it does demonstrate that the public narrative can be changed by the public itself, and altering

[*] Rich Morin, "Rising Share of Americans See Conflict Between Rich and Poor," Pew Research Center, January 11, 2012.

the narrative is a necessary victory on the way toward transforming everything else.

Part of the narrative shift has been to admit that millions of ordinary Americans suffer with poverty while the "free market" system adds to their misery by offering "financial products" that squeeze them even harder than everyone else. "The trick," writes Barbara Ehrenreich, "is to rob them in ways that are systematic, impersonal, and almost impossible to trace to individual perpetrators."* The combination of corporate predation and state neglect creates forms of social coercion and structural violence waged against what Chomsky calls the "precariat"—those who live a precarious existence at the periphery of society: the elderly, the poor and communities of color. "It's not the periphery anymore," writes Chomsky, "it's becoming a very substantial part of society."

In early 2012, for example, the *New York Times* published a front-page story about a retired couple in Dixfield, Maine, who had fallen behind on paying their heating bills. When, during the dead of winter, their back debt reached $700, the oil company threatened to cut them off,

---

* Barbara Ehrenreich, "Preying on the Poor: How Government and Corporations Use the Poor as Piggy Banks," Economic Hardship Reporting Project, economichardship.org, May 17, 2012.

knowing that doing so might literally kill two people. The oil man said he "agonized over his decision," and when he got off the phone with the couple he thought to himself, "Are these people going to be found frozen?"* But he cut them off anyway.

In the very same issue of the *Times*, just a few pages in, appears a column by Charles Blow discussing multimillionaire Mitt Romney's statement that he was "not concerned about the very poor," because there is a "safety net" for them. Blow responds to Romney's assurance with these words: "Where to begin? First, a report from the Center on Budget and Policy Priorities last month pointed out that Romney's budget proposals would take a chainsaw to that safety net."†

How did we in the United States get to this point? "It's not Third World misery," says Chomsky, "but it's not what it ought to be in a rich society, the richest in the world, in fact, with plenty of wealth around, which people can see, just not in their pockets." And Chomsky credits

---

* Dan Barry, "In Fuel Oil Country, Cold That Cuts to the Heart," *New York Times*, February 3, 2012.

† Charles M. Blow, "Romney, the Rich and the Rest," *New York Times*, February 3, 2012, citing Richard Kogan and Paul N. Van de Water, "Romney Budget Proposals Would Require Massive Cuts in Medicare, Medicaid, and Other Nondefense Spending," Center on Budget and Policy Priorities, revised February 16, 2012.

the work of movement organizers for having helped bring these issues to the fore and having initiated a shift.

While the organizing continues to move forward, media coverage of what's happening has not. In a May 23, 2012, article, Arun Gupta writes about how newspapers have drifted away from covering the movement and the unresolved issues that triggered it. "A study by two sociologists backs this up," writes Gupta. "Surveying more than 2,200 U.S. newspapers, Jackie Smith and Patrick Rafail found coverage of the Occupy movement has dwindled to a trickle since November, despite hundreds of active Occupy groups, thousands of organizing projects and extensive May Day activity. Even more telling, newspaper coverage of inequality has shrunk by nearly 70 per cent since autumn."* By 2013, national coverage of Occupy-related organizing went completely dark.

Despite the attention deficit from profit-driven media, nonprofit community institutions like *Democracy Now!*, Free Speech Radio News, *In These Times*, AlterNet and Waging Nonviolence not only continue to cover the issues but do so with an equal sense of urgency.

---

* Arun Gupta, "What happened to the Occupy movement?, www.aljazeera.com, May 23, 2012.

With or without occupied spaces, with or without the name "Occupy," across the nation ordinary people continue to organize and build on the movement's momentum, waging non-violent, increasingly creative actions in hundreds of cities. These include defending people and their homes from bank-ordered evictions and disrupting bank-organized auctions at which people's stolen homes are sold off to the highest bidder—actions which not only expose the poverty of the free market system but also offer meaningful solidarity to those the system robs and tramples. "As preexisting anti-foreclosure organizations and Occupy merge," writes Laura Gottesdiener, "the campaign is spreading to nearly every major city, with front-lawn occupations, eviction defense teams or auction blockades currently under way in Boston, Tampa, Maui, Detroit, Nashville, Birmingham, New York City, Washington, D.C., Chicago, Cleveland, Atlanta, Minneapolis, Delaware and cities across California."*

In addition to discussing foreclosure defense and worker takeovers, in *Occupy* Chomsky speaks to the many options and opportunities that exist to change the system, and he points to examples

---

* Laura Gottesdiener, "We win when we live here: occupying homes in Detroit and beyond," wagingnonviolence.org, March 28, 2012.

in which the movement's vision has already impacted city council proposals, debates and resolutions. One such case is New York City Council Resolution 1172, which formally opposes corporate personhood and calls for an amendment to the U.S. Constitution to permanently ban it. The resolution creates clear dividing lines between the rights of corporations and the rights of citizens, and it adds to the momentum produced by a growing list of cities—including Los Angeles, Oakland, Albany and Boulder—that have passed similar resolutions.*

What makes this all the more remarkable is that despite the "inevitable repression," as Chomsky calls it—the pushback of police brutality, mass arrests, trumped-up charges, restrictive city ordinances, coordinated surveillance, infiltration, raids and serious cases of entrapment—those who participated in the original occupations continue to organize, mounting new tactics on new fronts from inner-city neighborhoods and rural farms to the halls of Congress and the sidewalk in front of the White House. Simply continuing in the face of repression can be considered an achievement, and

---

* Bailey McCann, "Cities, states pass resolutions against corporate personhood," CivSource, January 4, 2012. http://civsourceonline.com/2012/01/04/cities-states-pass-resolutions-against-corporate-personhood

Chomsky considers the government surveillance and repression itself an indication of the people's widespread success.

Movement energy is derived, in part, from people's indignation with being ignored in the face of acute injustice. Watching billions of tax-collected dollars keep banks afloat while the very same banks evict people from their homes has roused the anger of millions. Watching billions more in tax-collected dollars gush to pay for wars and drone killings while politicians cut social services at home is equally appalling.

Economic injustice is the face of the problem; a political crisis in representational democracy underlies it. Many politicians, for example, no longer hide the fact that they do not have to answer to the people. During a Republican presidential debate moderated by CNN anchor Anderson Cooper, one of the candidates was asked an immigration-related question. When he ignored the question and rambled on about something else, Cooper pushed him to answer. Dismissing Cooper, the politician snarled, "You get to ask the questions, I get to answer like I want to," drawing loud boos from the live audience.*

---

* Emily Ramshaw and Jay Root, "A New Rick Perry Shows Up to GOP Debate," *Texas Tribune*, October 18, 2011. http://www.texastribune.org/texas-politics/2012-presidential-election/new-rick-perry-shows-gop-debate/

But booing isn't enough. Politicians' open defection from the public interest is precisely what has driven people from all walks of life to face tear gas, pepper spray, stun grenades, handcuffs and jail time in order to be heard. Spurred by indignation at politicians' failure to deliver anything but endless campaigns and vague promises, perhaps the movement's most radical message is its incitement to change ourselves, individually and collectively, in the workplace and across society as whole. Chomsky discusses this through advocacy of worker control and through discussion of the importance of redefining ideas like economic growth. If we continue to pursue the dominant model, he says, we'll be like "lemmings walking over a cliff." Instead, he encourages the movement to continue spreading ideas about "a different way of living" that is based not on maximizing how much we can buy, but on "maximizing values that are important for life." To expect elected officials to turn things around on their own is to go the way of the lemming. No one is going to do it for us. As the black feminist poet June Jordan said, "We are the ones we have been waiting for."

"How can we find ways to work together to overcome barriers and tensions and become part of a dedicated, ongoing, sustained movement which is going to last a long time?" asks Chomsky. *How can we get it together?*

In the new set of interviews presented here in the second edition, one word stands out: solidarity. Chomsky is not attached to occupying; it's just a tactic, he says, useful for a time, but not something to be attached to. "What really counts," says Chomsky, is "solidarity, mutual aid, care for one another." The intention of this pamphlet is to encourage that spirit, what the Zapatistas call *compañerismo*.

As Howard Zinn wrote, "Where progress has been made, wherever any kind of injustice has been overturned, it's been because people acted as citizens, and not as politicians. They didn't just moan. They worked, they acted, they organized, they rioted if necessary to bring their situation to the attention of people in power. And that's what we have to do today. Some people might say, 'Well, what do you expect?'

"And the answer is that we expect a lot.

"People say, 'What, are you a dreamer?'

"And the answer is yes, we're dreamers.

"We want it all. We want a peaceful world. We want an egalitarian world. We don't want war. We don't want capitalism. We want a decent society."

It is in that beautiful spirit, the spirit of Howard

Zinn and that of Zuccotti Park during the occupation, that we present this second edition of Noam Chomsky's *Occupy*.

—Greg Ruggiero
July 2013

OCCUPY YOUR HEART
ANOTHER WORLD IS POSSIBLE,
Make Ready your DREAMS
I still Can't EAT GNP
but i can SEE
CLIMATE CHANGE
UT MY WINDOW

Noam Chomsky addressing Occupy Boston in
Dewey Square, October 22, 2011.

OCCUPY

Howard Zinn Memorial Lecture

Occupy Boston, MA, Dewey Square, October 22, 2011

It's a little hard to give a Howard Zinn memorial lecture at an Occupy meeting. There are mixed feelings, necessarily, that go along with it. First of all, there's regret that Howard is not here to take part in and invigorate it in his inimitable way, something that would have been the dream of his life. Secondly, there is excitement that the dream is actually being fulfilled. It's a dream for which he laid a lot of the groundwork, and it would have been the fulfillment of a dream for him to have been here with you.

Whenever I think about Howard, which is quite often, particularly in light of the Occupy movement, there are words of his that always resonate in my mind. They are his call to focus our attention on "the countless small actions of unknown people" that are the foundation for "those great moments" that ultimately enter the historical record without the countless small actions of unknown people that created them. That's a fundamental truth of history. And it's one that his work, and in fact his life, did a great deal to illuminate.

It's no exaggeration to say that he literally changed the consciousness and also the conscience of an entire generation. It's no small achievement. And it continues and expands.

A Howard Zinn memorial lecture could not have been better timed. It's taking place in the midst of "countless small actions of unknown people" who are rising.

The Occupy movement is an extremely exciting development. In fact, it's kind of spectacular. It's unprecedented. There's never been anything like it that I can think of.

If the bonds and associations that are being established in these remarkable events can be sustained through a long, hard period ahead—because victory won't come quickly—it could turn out to be a really historic, and very significant, moment in American history.

The fact that the Occupy movement is unprecedented is quite appropriate. It's an unprecedented era. Not just this moment, but since the 1970s.

On the History of the U.S. Economy

The 1970s began a major turning point in American history. For centuries, since the country began, it had been a developing society, and not always in very pretty ways. That's another story, but it was a developing society, with ups and downs. But the general progress was towards wealth, industrialization, development, and hope. There was a pretty constant expectation that it was going to go on like this. That was true even in very dark times.

I'm just old enough to remember the Great Depression. After the first few years, by the mid-1930s—although the situation was objectively much harsher than it is today—nevertheless, the spirit was quite different. There was a sense that "we're gonna get out of it," even among unemployed people, including a lot of my relatives, a sense that "it will get better."

There was militant labor union organizing, especially CIO (Congress of Industrial Organizations), organizing going on. It was getting to the point of sit-down strikes, which are really very frightening to the business world—you could see it in the business press at the time—because a sit-down strike is just a step before taking over the factory and running it yourself. The idea of worker takeovers is something which is, incidentally, very much on the agenda today, and we should keep it in mind—I'll come back to it. Also the New Deal legislations were beginning to come in as a result of popular pressure. Despite the hard times, there was a sense that, somehow, "we're gonna get out of it."

It's quite different now. For many people in the United States, there's kind of a pervasive sense of hopelessness, sometimes despair. I think it's quite new in American history. And it has an objective basis.

On the Working Class

In the 1930s, unemployed working people could anticipate that their jobs would come back. If you're a worker in manufacturing today (the current level of unemployment in manufacturing is approximately like the Depression) and current tendencies persist, those jobs aren't going to come back.

The change took place in the 1970s. There are a lot of reasons for it. One of the underlying factors, discussed mainly by economic historian Robert Brenner, was the falling rate of profit in manufacturing. There were other factors. It led to major changes in the economy—a reversal of the several hundred years of progress towards industrialization and development and that turned to a process of de-industrialization and de-development. Of course, manufacturing production continued overseas—very profitable, but no good for the work force.

Along with that came a significant shift of the economy from productive enterprise—producing

things people need or could use—to financial manipulation. The financialization of the
economy really took off at that time.

On Banks

Before the 1970s, banks were banks. They did
what banks were supposed to do in a state capitalist economy: they took unused funds from your
bank account, for example, and transferred them
to some potentially useful purpose like helping
some family to buy a home or send a kid to college,
or whatever it might be. That changed dramatically
in the 1970s. Until then, there were no financial
crises. It was a period of enormous growth—the
highest growth in American history, maybe in
economic history—sustained growth through the
1950s and 1960s. And it was egalitarian.

So the lowest quintile did about as well as the
highest quintile. Lots of people moved into rea-
sonable lifestyles. What's called here "middle
class." "Working class," as it's called in other
countries. But it was real.

And the 1960s accelerated it. The activism of
the 1960s, after a pretty dismal decade, really civilized the country in lots of ways that are permanent. They're not changing. They're staying on.

When the 1970s came along there were sudden
and sharp changes: de-industrialization, off-

shoring of production, and shifting to financial institutions, which grew enormously. I should say that, in the 1950s and 1960s, there was also the development of what several decades later became the high-tech economy: computers, the Internet, the IT Revolution, mostly developed in the 1950s and 1960s, substantially in the state sector. It took a couple of decades before it took off, but it was developed there.

The developments that took place during the 1970s set off a vicious cycle. It led to concentration of wealth increasingly in the hands of the financial sector. This doesn't benefit the economy—it probably harms it and the society—but it did lead to tremendous concentration of wealth, substantially there.

On Politics and Money

Concentration of wealth yields concentration of political power. And concentration of political power gives rise to legislation that increases and accelerates the cycle. The legislation, essentially bipartisan, drives new fiscal policies, tax changes, also rules of corporate governance, and deregulation. Alongside of this began the very sharp rise in the costs of elections, which drives the political parties even deeper than before into the pockets of the corporate sector.

The parties dissolved, essentially, in many ways. It used to be that if a person in Congress hoped for a position such as a committee chair or some position of responsibility, he or she got it mainly through seniority and service. Within a couple of years, they started having to put money into the party coffers in order to get ahead, a topic studied mainly by Tom Ferguson. That just drove the whole system even deeper into the pockets of the corporate sector, increasingly the financial sector.

This cycle resulted in a tremendous concentration of wealth, mainly in the top tenth of one percent of the population. Meanwhile, for the general population, it began to open a period of stagnation or even decline for the majority. People got by, but by artificial means such as longer working hours, high rates of borrowing and debt, and reliance on asset inflation like the recent housing bubble. Pretty soon those working hours were much higher in the United States than in other industrial countries like Japan and those in Europe. So there was a period of stagnation and decline for the majority that continued alongside a period of sharp concentration of wealth. The political system began to dissolve.

There has always been a gap between public policy and public will, but it just grew astronomically. You can see it right now, in fact.

Take a look at what's happening right now.

The big topic in Washington that everyone con-
centrates on is the deficit. For the public, correctly, the deficit is not regarded as much of an
issue. And it isn't really much of an issue. The
issue is joblessness, not the deficit. There's a deficit commission but there's no joblessness commission. As far as the deficit is concerned, the
public has opinions. Take a look at the polls. The
public overwhelmingly supports higher taxes on
the wealthy, which have declined sharply in this
period of stagnation and decline—higher taxes
on the wealthy and preserve the limited social
benefits.

The outcome of the deficit commission is
probably going to be the opposite. Either they'll
reach an agreement, which will be the opposite of
what the public wants, or else it will go into a kind
of automatic procedure that is going to have those
effects. Actually, that's something that has to be
dealt with very quickly.

The deficit commission is going to come up
with its decision in a couple of weeks. The Occupy
movements could provide a mass base for trying
to avert what amounts to a dagger pointed at the
heart of the country. It could have very negative
effects. It's an immediate task.

On Economics

Without going into details, what's been playing out for the past thirty years is actually a nightmare that was anticipated by the classical economists.

Adam Smith considered the possibility that merchants and manufacturers in England might decide to do their business abroad—invest abroad and import from abroad. He said they would profit, but England would be harmed.

However, he went on to say that the merchants and manufacturers would prefer to operate in their own country—what's sometimes called a "home bias." So, as if by "an invisible hand," England would be saved from the ravages of what is now called neoliberal globalization. That's a pretty hard passage to miss. In his classic *Wealth of Nations*, that's the only occurrence of the phrase, "invisible hand." Maybe England would be saved from neoliberal globalization by an "invisible hand."

The other great classical economist, David Ricardo, recognized the same thing and hoped that it wouldn't happen—kind of a sentimental hope—and it didn't for a long time. But now it is happening. Over the last thirty years that's exactly what has been underway.

Plutonomy and the Precariat

For the general population, the 99 percent in the imagery of the Occupy movement, it's been pretty harsh. And it could get worse. This could be a period of irreversible decline. For the 1 percent and even less—the one-tenth of the 1 percent— it's just fine. They are richer than ever, more powerful than ever, controlling the political system, disregarding the public. And if it can continue, as far as they're concerned, sure, why not? Just what Adam Smith and David Ricardo warned about.

Take, for example, Citigroup. For decades, Citigroup has been one of the most corrupt of the major investment banking corporations, repeatedly bailed out by the taxpayer, starting in the early Reagan years and now once again. I won't run through the corruption—you probably already know about it—but it's pretty astonishing.

In 2005, Citigroup came out with a brochure for investors called "Plutonomy: Buying Luxury, Explaining Global Imbalances." The brochure urged investors to put money into a "plutonomy index." The memo says "the World is dividing into two blocs - the Plutonomy and the rest."

Plutonomy refers to the rich, those who buy luxury goods and so on, and that's where the action is. They said that their plutonomy index was way out-performing the stock market, so people should put money into it. As for the rest, we send 'em adrift. We don't really care about them. We don't really need 'em. They have to be around to provide a powerful state, which will protect us and bail us out when we get into trouble, but other than that they essentially have no function. These days they're sometimes called the "precariat"—people who live a precarious existence at the periphery of society. It's not the periphery anymore. It's becoming a very substantial part of the society in the United States, and indeed elsewhere. And this is considered a good thing.

So, for example, Alan Greenspan, at the time when he was still "Saint Alan"—hailed by the economics profession as one of the greatest economists of all time (this was before the crash for which he was substantially responsible)—was testifying to Congress in the Clinton years, and he explained the wonders of the great economy that he was supervising. He said a lot of the success of this economy was based substantially on what he called "growing worker insecurity." If working people are insecure, if they're part of what we now call the "precariat," living precarious existences, they're not going to make demands, they're not going to try to get wages, they won't get benefits. We can kick 'em out if we don't need 'em. And that's what's called a "healthy" economy, technically. And he was very highly praised for this, greatly admired.

Well, now the world is indeed splitting into a plutonomy and a precariat—again, in the imagery of the Occupy movement, the 1 percent and the 99 percent. Not literal numbers, but the right picture. Now, the plutonomy is where the action is. Well, it could continue like this.

If it does continue like this, the historic reversal that began in the 1970s could become irreversible. That's where we're heading. And the Occupy movement is the first real, major popular reaction that could avert this. But, as I said, it's going to be necessary to face the fact that it's a long, hard struggle. You don't win victories tomorrow. You have to go on, have to form the structures that will be sustained, that will go on through hard times and can win major victories. And there are a lot of things that can be done.

Toward Worker Takeover

I mentioned before that, in the 1930s, one of the most effective actions was the sit-down strike. And the reason is very simple: that's just a step before takeover of the industry.

Through the 1970s, as the decline was setting in, there were some very important events that took place. One was in the late '70s. In 1977, U.S.

Steel decided to close one of its major facilities in Youngstown, Ohio. Instead of just walking away, the workforce and the community decided to get together and buy it from U.S. Steel, hand it over to the work force, and turn it into a worker-run, worker-managed facility. They didn't win. But, with enough popular support, they could have won. It was a partial victory. It's a topic that Gar Alperovitz and Staughton Lynd—the lawyer for the workers and community—have discussed in detail.

It was a partial victory because, even though they lost, it set off other efforts. And now, throughout Ohio, and in fact in other places, there's a scattering of hundreds, maybe thousands, of sometimes not-so-small worker/community-owned industries that could become worker-managed. And that's the basis for a real revolution. That's how it takes place. It's happening here, too.

In one of the suburbs of Boston, about a year ago, something similar happened. A multinational decided to close down a profitable, functioning manufacturing facility carrying out some high-tech manufacturing. Evidently, it just wasn't profitable enough for them. The workforce and the union offered to buy it, take it over, and run it themselves. The multinational decided to close it down instead, probably for reasons of class-consciousness. I don't think they want things like this to happen. If there had been enough popular support, if there had been something like this movement that could have gotten involved, they might have succeeded.

And there are other things going on like that. In fact, some of them are major. Not long ago, Obama took over the auto industry, which was basically owned by the public. And there were a number of things that could have been done. One was what was done: reconstitute it so that it can be handed back to the ownership, or very similar ownership, and continue on its traditional path.

The other possibility was to hand it over to the workforce—which owned it anyway—turn it into a worker-owned, worker-managed major industrial system that's a big part of the economy, and have it produce things that people need. And there's a lot that we need.

We all know or should know that the United States is extremely backward globally in high-speed transportation, and it's very serious. It not only affects people's lives, but it affects the economy.

In that regard, here's a personal story. I happened to be giving talks in France a couple of months ago and ended up in Southern France and had to take a train from Avignon to Charles De Gaulle Airport in Paris. It took two hours. The trip we took was the same distance as from Washington, DC, to Boston. I don't know if you've ever taken the train from Washington to Boston, but it's operating at about the same speed it was sixty years ago when my wife and I first took it. It's a scandal. It could be done here as it's been done in Europe. They had the capacity to do it, the skilled work force. It would have taken a little popular support, but it could have made a major change in the economy.

Just to make it more surreal, while this option was being avoided, the Obama administration was sending its transportation secretary to Spain to get contracts for developing high-speed rail for the United States, which could have been done right in the Rust Belt, which is being closed down. There are no economic reasons why this can't happen. These are class reasons, and reflect the lack of popular political mobilization. Things like this continue.

Climate Change and Nuclear Weapons

Let me just say that I've kept to domestic issues, and these are by no means the only ones. You all know that. There are very dangerous developments in the international arena, including two of them, which are a kind of a shadow that hangs over everything we've discussed. There are, for the first time in human history, real threats to decent survival of the species.

Two are particularly urgent. One has been hanging around since 1945. It's kind of a miracle that we've escaped it. That's the threat of nuclear war and nuclear weapons. Though it isn't being much discussed, that threat is in fact being escalated by policies of this administration and its allies. And something has to be done about that or we're in real trouble.

The other, of course, is environmental catastrophe. Practically every country in the world is taking at least halting steps towards trying to do something about it. The United States is also taking steps, mainly to accelerate the threat.

The United States is the only major country that is not only not doing something constructive to protect the environment. It's not climbing on the train. In some ways it's pulling it backwards.

Congress right now is dismantling legislation instituted by Richard Nixon—really the last liberal president of the U.S., literally, and that shows you what's been going on. They're dismantling the limited measures of the Nixon administration to try to do something about what is a growing, emerging catastrophe.

And this is connected with a huge propaganda system, proudly and openly declared by the business world, to try to convince people that climate change is just a liberal hoax. "Why pay attention to these scientists?" And we're really regressing back to the medieval period. It's not a joke.

If that's happening in the most powerful, richest country in history, then this catastrophe isn't going to be averted. And everything else we're talking about won't matter in a generation or two. All that is going on right now. Something has to be done about it very soon, in a dedicated, sustained way.

It's not going to be easy to proceed. There are going to be barriers, difficulties, hardships, failures—it's inevitable. But unless the process that is taking place here and elsewhere in the country and around the world, unless that continues to grow and to become a major force in the social and political world, the chances for a decent future are not very high.

QUESTIONS FROM OCCUPY BOSTON

Regarding fixing political dysfunction in this country, what about enacting a Constitutional amendment to abolish corporate personhood or to get corporate money out of politics?

These would be very good things to do, but you can't do this or anything else unless there is a large, active, popular base. If the Occupy movement was the leading force in the country, you could push many things forward.

But remember, most people don't know that this is happening. Or they may know it is happening, but don't know what it is. And among those who do know, polls show that there's a lot of support.

That assigns a task. It's necessary to get out into the country and get people to understand what this is about, and what they can do about it, and what the consequences are of not doing anything about it.

Corporate personhood is an important case in point, but pay attention to what it is. We should think about it. We're supposed to worship the U.S. Constitution these days. The Fifth Amendment says that "no person shall be deprived" of rights "without due process of law." Well, by "person," the Founding Fathers didn't actually mean "person." So, for example, there were a lot of creatures of flesh and blood that weren't considered to be "persons." The indigenous population, for example. They didn't have any rights. In the U.S. Constitution there was a category of creatures called three-fifth humans—the enslaved population. They weren't considered persons. And in fact women were barely considered persons, so they didn't have rights.

A lot of this was somewhat rectified over the years. After the Civil War, the Fourteenth Amendment raised the three-fifths humans to full humans, at least in principle. But that was only in principle. Soon other methods were instituted to criminalize Black life, which led to virtual restoration of a kind of slavery. In fact, something like that is happening again now, as the processes of neoliberal globalization I was talking about leave a superfluous population among the precariat; and with the fairly close class-race-ethnicity relation in the United States, that means largely Black, secondarily Hispanic.

Over the following years, the concept of "person" was changed by the courts in two ways. One way was to broaden it to include corporations, legal fictions established and sustained by the state. In fact, these "persons" later became the management of corporations, according to the court decisions. So the management of corporations became "persons."

It was also narrowed to exclude undocumented immigrants. They had to be excluded from the category of "persons." And that's happening right now. So the legislations that you're talking about, they go two ways. They broaden the category of persons to include corporate entities, which now have rights way beyond human beings, given by the trade agreements and others, and they exclude the people who flee from Central America where the U.S. devastated their homelands, and flee from Mexico because they can't compete with the highly-subsidized U.S. agribusiness.

Remember that, when NAFTA was passed in 1994, the Clinton administration understood pretty well that it was going to devastate the Mexican economy, and that's the year when they started militarizing the border. Well, now we're getting the consequences, and these people have to be excluded from the category of persons. So when you talk about personhood—that's right— but there's more than one aspect to it, and it ought to be pushed forward and all of it understood and acted upon.

That requires a mass base. It requires that the population understands this and is committed to it. It's easy to think of things that need to be done, but they all have a prerequisite, namely, a mass popular base that is committed to implementing it.

How likely is it that the ruling class in America could develop an openly fascist system here?

I think it's very unlikely, frankly. They don't have the force. About a century ago, in the freest countries in the world at that time—Britain and the United States—the dominant classes came to understand that they can't control the population by force any longer. Too much freedom had been won by struggles like these. They realized this, they were self-conscious about it, and it's discussed in their literature.

The dominant class recognized they had to shift their tactics to control of attitudes and beliefs instead of just the cudgel. They didn't throw away the cudgel, but it can't do what it used to do. You have to control attitudes and beliefs. In fact, that's when the public relations industry began. It began in the United States and England, the free countries where you had to have a major industry to control beliefs and attitudes; to induce consumerism, passivity, apathy, distraction—all the things you know very well. And that's the way it's been going on. It's a barrier, but it's a lot easier to overcome than torture and the Gestapo. I don't think the circumstances exist any longer for instituting anything like what we called fascism.

Sir, I have a two-part question that I've been waiting to ask you my whole life. You mentioned earlier that sit-down protests are just a precursor to a takeover of industry. I'd like to ask you if, today, you would advocate a general strike as an effective tactic for moving forward; and second, would you ever, if asked, allow for your voice to relay the democratically chosen will of our nation?

My voice wouldn't help. And besides, you don't want leaders; you want to do it yourselves. [Applause and cheers] We need representation, but you need to pick them yourselves and they need to be recallable representatives. We're not going to fall into some system of control and hierarchy.

But the question of the general strike is like the others. You can think of it as a possible idea at a time when the population is ready for it. We can't sit here and just declare a general strike. Obviously, there has to be approval, agreement, and willingness to take the risks to participate on the part of the large mass the population. There has to be organization, education, activism. Education doesn't mean just telling people what to believe. It means learning things for ourselves.

There is a famous line by Karl Marx, which I am sure many of you know: the task is not just to understand the world, but to change it. And there is a variant of that which should also be kept in mind. If you want to change the world in a constructive direction, you better try to understand it first. And understanding it doesn't mean just listening to a talk or reading a book, although that's helpful sometimes. It means learning. And you learn through participation. You learn from others. You learn from the people you are trying to organize. And you have to gain the experience and understanding which will make it possible to maybe implement ideas like that as a tactic.

But there is a long way to go, and you don't get there by a flick of the wrist. That happens by hard, long-term, dedicated work.

And I think that maybe, in many ways, the most exciting aspect of the Occupy movement is the construction of the associations, bonds, linkages and networks that are taking place all over—whether it's a collaborative kitchen or something else. And, out of that, if it can be sustained and expanded to a large part of the population who doesn't yet know what is going on. If that can happen, then you can raise questions about tactics like a general strike that could very well at some point be appropriate.

We have two questions about Occupy worldwide: First, how do you think we can effectively target problems to bring about change? And should we make demands?

They should have proposals and ideas, and there doesn't have to be agreement on them. There's good reason to "let a hundred flowers bloom." There are lots of possibilities, but there are very sensible proposals, starting from very short-term ones. Let's prevent the deficit commission from carrying out a very lethal blow against society that might have lasting effects in the next couple of weeks. That's pretty short-term.

There are longer-terms things, like the ones I mentioned—helping the workforce in the Boston suburb I mentioned to take over their own industry, instead of becoming jobless. Then going on to maybe do the same thing with the whole manufacturing industry. And there are many things like that coming along.

Turning the country into a leader in the effort to try to mitigate—maybe overcome—the tremendous threat of global warming, instead of being a follower in that regard, or in fact a leader, and practically the only participant, in the campaign to accelerate the threat.

All of those are things that you can do. We should have those proposals. Dealing with corporate personhood is another proposal, but I would suggest that it be broadened to deal with the distortion—the gross distortion—in the concept of person, which both broadens it to include corporate entities and narrows it to exclude legally defined non-people. And there are plenty of other demands I could think of. They should be formulated. Not everyone has to agree on the ranking of priorities or even the choice of demands, but groups can pursue them. There is a lot that can be done.

Should we rewrite the system? How can we mobilize the American public?

The only way to mobilize the American public that I've ever heard of—or any other public— is by going out and joining them. Going out to wherever people are—churches, clubs, schools, unions—wherever they may be. Getting involved with them and trying to learn from them and to bring about a change of consciousness among them. And, again, this can be very concrete.

Let's take the electoral system in the United States. It has a lot of flaws—like what I mentioned: public policy and public opinion are so radically divorced. But there are some narrower things that you can do something about right away.

We're coming up to the presidential election's primary season. Suppose we had a functioning democratic society. Let's just imagine that. What would a primary look like, say, in New Hampshire? What would happen in a primary would be that the people in a town would get together and discuss, talk about, and argue about what they want policy to be. Sort of like what's been happening here in the Occupy movement. They should formulate a conception of what the policy should be. Then if a candidate comes along and says, "I want to come talk to you," the people in the town ought to say, "Well, you can come listen to us if you want. So you come in, we'll tell you what we want, and you can try to persuade us that you'll do it; then, maybe we will vote for you." That's what would happen in a democratic society.

What happens in our society? The candidate comes to town with his public relations agents and the rest of them. He gives some talks, and says,

"Look how great I am. This is what I am going to do for you." Anybody with a grey-cell functioning doesn't believe a word he or she says. And then maybe people vote for him, maybe they don't. That's very different from a democratic society.

Making moves in the direction of real democracy is not utopian. Those are things that can be done in particular communities. And it could lead to a noticeable change in the political system.

Sure, we should get money out of politics, but that's going to take a lot of work. One way to go at it is just to elect your own representatives. It's not impossible. The same is true all across the board.

Let's go back to the deficit again. The population understands that it's not the primary problem. In fact, it's not even a major problem. The population has a sensible attitude about what ought to be done with it, like higher taxes for the rich and going back to the way things were during the big growth periods and preserving the benefits—they're limited, and they ought to be improved.

And there's something else that isn't even being discussed. The deficit would be eliminated, literally, if the United States had a health care system of a kind that other industrial countries have. [Loud applause] You know, that's literally true. It's not utopian. The idea that we should have health care like other industrial countries is not wild radical raving. [Laughter]

The health care system in the United States, I'm sure you know, is a total international scandal. It's twice the per capita cost of comparable countries and one of the worst outcomes, with a huge number of people uninsured altogether. And it's going to get worse.

The problem is not Medicare. Medicare is indeed a problem, but it's a problem because it goes through the privatized, largely unregulated system that is totally dysfunctional.

You can't talk about this in Washington because of the power of financial institutions. A large part of the public wants it. In fact, for decades substantial parts of the population, often big majorities, have been in favor of this, but it can't be talked about. There's too much power now in the financial institutions. But that can be changed. It's not pie in the sky. And to the extent that the deficit is a problem, that's one thing that can be done about it.

The other thing that can be done, you all know about: reining in our crazed military system, which has about the same expenses as the militaries of the rest of the world combined. But our military system is not for defense. In fact, it's actually harmful to us, if you look at it. It doesn't have to be like that.

So there are things that are quite feasible. Proposals have to be made and brought to the population in a convincing way. And most of the population already agrees with most these things. But you have to turn the population into a force that will be active and engaged. Then you could have results.

Professor Chomsky, what are your thoughts on publicly financed campaigns?

Occupy Facilitator: I also have two points of information. This presentation is on the live stream and will be recorded and posted to occupyboston.org.

Another point of information is that there is now "Occupy Congress." Look for it on the Web. It's very new. Let's just do it!

Well, I think that's a pretty good answer to the question about what we should do about publicly financed campaigns: Let's just do it. We pick our own representatives. We finance them. We vote for them. If the corporations pour money into somebody else's pockets, they can spend it on luxury goods. That can be done, but only if you have an organized and engaged public.

There are lots of things you can propose. They all go back to the same basic conclusion: You have to have an organized, dedicated public that is willing to implement them. If there is, a lot of options open up, including these.

Could you please share your thoughts on the significance of the Occupy the 'Hood movement, and any insights you may have regarding cross-cultural organization for social change?

That's a great movement. I heard, just coming out here this evening, that the first Occupy the 'Hood action took place just yesterday in Boston. And it's been happening in other places, New York, and elsewhere.

That's perfect. It's just the kind of reaching out in the general community that makes sense. People have to do it themselves. I can't tell people at an Occupy in Roxbury what to do, and if I did, they shouldn't listen to me. They know how to do it.

We should work hard to get this integrated. And that means again, not just telling people "here's what you should believe," but learning from them. What do they want? What do they need? What can we learn from them? How can we find ways to work together to overcome barriers and tensions and become part of a dedicated, ongoing, sustained movement which is going to last a long time?

Most of these goals that we are talking about cannot be attained in a couple of weeks or months—actually some of them can—but most of them involve a long struggle.

People with power don't give it up unless they have to. And that takes work.

AFTER THIRTY YEARS OF CLASS WAR

Interview with Edward Radzivilovskiy, Student, New York University, Paris

Interview conducted at MIT, Cambridge, Massachusetts, January 6, 2012

I want to start off with something you said at Occupy Boston: "The most exciting aspect of the Occupy movement is the construction of the linkages that are taking place all over. If they can be sustained and expanded, Occupy can lead to dedicated efforts to set society on a more humane course."*

Some have said that the Occupy movement does not have a cohesive message of its demands. If you do believe that the Occupy movement does have specific demands, how many of these demands do you actually think can be realized?

There is quite a range of people from many walks of life and many concerns involved in the Occupy

---

* Noam Chomsky, "Occupy the Future," *inthesetimes.com*, November 1, 2011, http://www.inthesetimes.com/article/12206/occupy_the_future/.

movement. There are some general things that bring them together, but of course they all have specific concerns as well.

Primarily, I think this should be regarded as a response, the first major public response, in fact, to about thirty years of a really quite bitter class war that has led to social, economic and political arrangements in which the system of democracy has been shredded.

Congress, for example, has its lowest approval level in history—practically invisible—and other institutions' ratings are not much higher.

The population is angry, frustrated, bitter—and for good reasons. For the past generation, policies have been initiated that have led to an extremely sharp concentration of wealth in a tiny sector of the population. In fact, the wealth distribution is very heavily weighted by, literally, the top tenth of one percent of the population, a fraction so small that they're not even picked up on the census. You have to do statistical analysis just to detect them. And they have benefited enormously. This is mostly from the financial sector—hedge fund managers, CEOs of financial corporations, and so on.

At the same time, for the majority of the population, incomes have pretty much stagnated. Real wages have also stagnated, sometimes declined. The benefits system that was very strong has been weakened.

People have been getting by in the United States by much higher workloads, by debt which sooner or later becomes unsustainable, and by the illusions created by bubbles—most recently, the housing bubble which collapsed, like bubbles do, leaving about $8 trillion in paper wealth disappearing for some sectors of the population. So, by now, U.S. workers put in far more hours than their counterparts in other industrial countries, and for African Americans almost all wealth has disappeared. It has been a pretty harsh and bitter period—not by the standards of developing nations, but this is a rich society and people judge their situation and their prospects by what *ought* to be the case.

At the same time, concentration of wealth leads almost reflexively to concentration of political power, which in turn translates into legislation, naturally in the interests of those implementing it; and that accelerates what has been a vicious cycle leading to, as I said, bitterness, anger, frustration and a very atomized society. That's why the linkages in the Occupy movement are so important.

Occupy is really the first sustained response to this. People have referred to the Tea Party as a response, but that is highly misleading. The Tea Party is relatively affluent, white. Its influence and power come from the fact that it has enormous corporate support and heavy finance. Parts of the corporate world simply see them as their shock troops, but it's not a movement in the serious sense that Occupy is.

Going back to your question about the movement's demands, there are general ones that are very widely shared in the population: Concern about the inequality. Concern about the chicanery of the financial institutions and the way their influence on the government has led to a situation in which those responsible for the crisis are helped out, bailed out—richer and more powerful than ever, while the victims are ignored. There are very specific proposals concerning the regulation of financial transaction taxes, reversal of the rules of corporate governance that have led to this kind of situation: for example, a shifting of the tax code back to something more like what it used to be when the very rich were not essentially exempted from taxes, and many other quite specific demands of that kind. It goes on to include the interests of groups and their particular concerns, some of which are quite far reaching.

But I think, if you investigate the Occupy movements and you ask them what are their demands, they are reticent to answer and rightly so, because they are essentially crafting a point of view from many disparate sources. And one of the striking features of the movement has simply been the creation of cooperative communities—something very much lacking in an atomized, disintegrated society—that include general assemblies that carry out extensive discussion, kitchens, libraries, support systems, and so on. All of that is a work in progress leading to community structures that, if they can spread out into the broader community and retain their vitality, could be very important.

Colin Asher, a journalist, wrote a piece for The Progressive, *in which he says, "Most scribes have settled on the idea that Occupy Wall Street is like Tahrir Square in Egypt, but I disagree. Occupy Wall Street is more like a Hooverville. The space itself engages people's imaginations, but nothing will be settled here, not even the meaning of what is happening, and the participants won't be able to define it. It matters that something is happening in lower Manhattan, and that people are paying attention, but it doesn't much matter what is happening."**

And you have said, "The 2012 election is now expected to cost two billion dollars. It's going to have to be mostly corporate funding. So it's not at all surprising that Obama is selecting business leaders for top positions. The public is quite angry and frus-

---

* Colin Asher, "Occupy Wall St. in NYC—The Week That Was," *The Progressive*, October 16, 2011.

trated, but unless Western populations can rise to the level of Egyptians they're going to remain victims."

So what I am wondering is, do you see the Occupy movement as an anarchist movement—the kind of uprising you have been advocating for most of your career? Is it a precursor to a revolution, or can these goals be achieved without a revolution?

First of all, let's talk about Egypt. What happened in Tahrir Square was extremely important, of historic importance in fact, and it did achieve a goal, namely, eliminating the dictatorship. But it left the regime in power. So yes, that's an important goal and there have been achievements: the press is much freer and the labor activism is much less constrained.

In fact, one striking difference between the Egyptian and Tunisian uprisings and the Occupy movements is that, in the North African case, the labor movement was right at the center of it. And, in fact, there is a very close correlation between such successes as there have been in the Middle East and North Africa and the level of labor militancy there over many years. That's been true in Egypt for years. They're usually crushed, but

---

* Noam Chomsky, "The State-Corporate Complex: A Threat to Freedom and Survival," lecture given at the University of Toronto, April 7, 2011. http://chomsky.info/talks/20110407.htm.

some successes. As soon as the labor movement became integrated into the April 6 movement—the Tahrir Square movement—it became a really significant and powerful force.

That's quite different here. The labor movement has been decimated. Part of the task to be carried out is to revitalize it.

In Tunisia they did succeed in getting rid of a dictator and in running a parliamentary election, now with a moderate Islamist party in control.

In Egypt, as I said, there were gains, but the military-run regime is very much in power. There will be a parliamentary election; there has been already. The groups that are succeeding in the elections are those that have been working for years organizing among the general population—the Muslim Brotherhood and the Salafists.

It's quite a different situation here. There hasn't been that kind of large-scale organizing. The labor movement has been struggling to retain victories that it won a long time ago and that it has been losing.

To have a revolution—a meaningful one—you need a substantial majority of the population who recognize or believe that further reform is not possible within the institutional framework that exists. And there is nothing like that here, not even remotely.

Should we be trying to achieve that? Should we be working up to a revolution or should we be trying to achieve it some other way?

First of all, we are nowhere near the limits of what reform can carry out. People can have the idea of a revolution in the back of their minds if they want. But there are very substantive actions that should be taking place.

I don't exactly know what it means to say, "*Is this just anarchist?*" Anarchist movements are very concerned with achieving specific goals. That's what they have traditionally been and that's what they should be. In this case, as I said, there are very specific short-term goals that have large support: fiscal policy, controlling financial institutions, dealing with environmental problems which are extraordinarily significant, shifting the political systems so that elections are not simply blocked, and so on. All of these are very direct and immediate concerns.

For example, just a couple of days ago, New York City's City Council, probably under the influence of the Occupy movement, passed a resolution, unanimously I think, against corporate personhood. The resolution establishes that "corporations are not entitled to the entirety of protections or 'rights' of natural persons, specifically so that the expenditure of corporate money to influence the electoral process is no longer a form of constitutionally protected speech" and calls on Congress "to begin the process of amending the Constitution."*

Well, that's pretty far reaching. It's a very popular idea in this country, and if it's pursued, it will dismantle a century of judicial decisions that have given corporations and state-created fictitious legal entities extraordinary rights and power. The population doesn't like it and has a right not to like it. Such steps are already being taken in words and could lead to action.

In the longer term, there are many things that can be done. For example, in many parts of the country, particularly Ohio, there's quite a significant spread of worker-owned enterprises. As I mentioned to Occupy Boston, a lot of this derived from a major effort, over thirty years ago, when U.S. Steel wanted to sell off and close one of its major installations. The work force and the community offered to buy it and run it themselves— industrial democracy, essentially. That went to the courts and they lost, although with sufficient support they could have won. But even the failure, like many failures, has spawned other efforts. Now there's a network of worker/community-owned enterprises spreading over the region.

---

* New York City Council, Resolution 1172, January 4, 2012.

Is this reform or revolution? If it extends, it's revolution. It changes the institutional structure of the society. Actually, a lot of it is supported by conservatives. It doesn't break very simply or sharply on what's called, mostly meaninglessly, a right-left spectrum. But these are things that respond to people's needs and concerns. There are cases right near here where similar options were possible. And I think those are directions that should definitely be pursued. A lot of these struggles are invigorated by things like the Occupy movement.

Similarly, going back to Egypt where the situation is quite different, they have very immediate concerns, like the question of what will the power of the military regime be. Will it be replaced by Islamist forces based in the slums and rural areas? What place will secular liberal elements—the ones who actually initiated the Tahrir Square demonstrations—find in this system? These are all very concrete problems that they have to deal with. Here, there are different concrete problems to deal with. There are many similarities.

In both cases, in Egypt and the United States, and in fact much the world, what's happening is a reaction—in my opinion a much-too-delayed reaction—to the neoliberal policies of roughly the last thirty years. They have been implemented in different ways in different countries. But it's generally the case that, to the extent that they have been implemented everywhere, they have been harmful to the general population and beneficial to a very small sector. And that's not accidental.

There is a new small book by the Economic Policy Institute called *Failure by Design: The Story behind America's Broken Economy*. And the phrase, "by design," is accurate. These things don't happen by the laws of nature or by principles of economics, to the extent they exist. They're choices. And they are choices made by the wealthy and powerful elements to create a society that answers to their needs. It's happened, and it's happening in Europe right now.

Take the European Central Bank (ECB). There are many economists, Nobel Laureates and others, and I agree with them, who think that the policies that the ECB is following and pursuing— basically austerity in a period of recession—are guaranteed to make the situation worse. So far, I think that's been the case.

Growth is what is needed in a period of recession, not austerity. Europe has the resources to stimulate growth, but their resources are not being used because of the policies of the Central Bank and others. And one can ask what the purpose of this is. And a rational way to judge purposes is to look at predictable consequences. And one consequence is that these policies undermine the social-democratic structures and the welfare-state structure that have been developed; they undermine the power of labor and create a more inegalitarian society, with greater power in the hands of the corporate sector and the wealthy. So it's class war basically, and that's a kind of "failure by design" as well.

I think a lot of people today, when you mention to them an anarchist society, they get the wrong impression. . . . Would you describe anarchist society as an ultra-radical version of democracy?

First of all, nobody owns the concept of "anarchism." Anarchism has a very broad back. You can find all kinds of things in the anarchist movements. So the question of what an anarchist society can be is almost meaningless. Different people who associate themselves with rough anarchist tendencies have very different conceptions.

But the most developed notions that anarchist activists and thinkers have had in mind are those for a highly organized society—highly structured, highly organized—but organized on the basis of free and voluntary participation. So, for example, what I mentioned about the Ohio network of worker/community-owned enterprises, that's a traditional anarchist vision. Enterprises, not only owned but *managed* by participants in a free association with one another is a big step beyond. It could be at the federal level. It could be at the international level. So yes, it's a highly democratic conception of a structured, organized society with power at the base. It doesn't mean that it doesn't have representatives—it can have, but they should be recallable and under the influence and control of participants.

Who's in favor of a society like that? You can say Adam Smith, for example, who believed—you can question whether his beliefs were accurate, but he *believed*—that market systems and the "invisible hand" of individual choices would lead to egalitarian societies of common participation. You can question the logic of the argument, but the goals are understandable and they go far back. You can find them in the first serious book of politics that was ever written, Aristotle's *Politics*.

When Aristotle evaluated various kinds of systems, he felt that democracy was the least bad of them. But he said democracy wouldn't work unless you could set things up so that they would be relatively egalitarian. He proposed specific measures for Athens that, in our terms, would be welfare-state measures.

There are plenty of roots for these concepts. A lot of them come right out of the Enlightenment. But I don't think anyone has the authority to say *this is what an anarchist society is going to look like.* There are people who think you can sketch it out in great detail, but my own feeling here—I essentially agree with Marx—is that these things have to be worked out by people who are living and functioning in freedom and work out for themselves what kinds of societies and communities are appropriate for them.

The late British philosopher, Martin Hollis, worked extensively on questions of human action, the philosophy of social science and rationality. One of the claims he made was that any anarchist vision of a society rests upon an idea of human nature that is too optimistic. In short, he argued that anarchism is only viable if humans by nature are good. He says that history shows us that humans cannot be trusted to this degree; thus, anarchism is too idealistic. Would you mind responding to this objection very quickly, given your commitment to some of the ideals of anarchism?

It's possible to respond to arguments. It is not possible to respond to opinions. If someone makes an assertion saying, "Here's what I believe," that's fine—he can say what he believes, but you can't respond to it. You can ask, what is the basis for your belief? Or, can you provide me with some evidence? What do you know about human nature?

Actually, we don't know very much about human nature. So yes, that's an expression of his belief, and he's entitled to make it. We have no idea, nor does he have any idea, if it's true or false. But it really doesn't matter; whatever the truth turns out to be, we will follow the same policies, namely, trying to optimize and maximize freedom, justice, participation, democracy. Those are goals that we'll attempt to realize. Maybe human beings are such that there's a limit to how far they can be realized; okay, we'll still follow the same policies. So, whatever one's un-argued assertions may be, it has very little effect on the policy and choices.

Professor Chomsky, thank you very much.

INTEROCCUPY

*InterOccupy conference call with Noam Chomsky,
Mikal Kamil and Ian Escuela, and questions submitted in
advance by others involved with Occupy, January 31, 2012.
InterOccupy.org provides channels of communications between general
assemblies, working groups and supporters across the Occupy movement.*

Professor Chomsky, the Occupy movement is in its second phase. Three of our main goals are to: 1) occupy the mainstream and transition from the tents and into the hearts and the minds of the masses; 2) block the repression of the movement by protecting the right of the 99 percent's freedom of assembly and right to speak without being violently attacked; and 3) end corporate personhood. The three goals overlap and are interdependent.

We are interested in learning what your position is on mainstream filtering, the repression of civil liberties, and the role of money and politics as they relate to Occupy and the future of America.

Coverage of Occupy has been mixed. At first it was dismissive, making fun of people involved as if they were just silly kids playing games and so on. But coverage changed. In fact, one of the really remarkable and almost spectacular successes of the Occupy movement is that it has simply changed the entire framework of discussion of many issues. There were things that were sort of known, but in the margins, hidden, which are now right up front—like the imagery of the 99 percent and 1 percent; and the dramatic facts of sharply rising inequality over the past roughly thirty years, with wealth being concentrated in actually a small fraction of 1 percent of the population. This has made a very heavy impact on the ridiculous maldistribution of wealth.

For the majority, real incomes have pretty much stagnated, sometimes declined. Benefits have also declined and work hours have gone up, and so on. It's not Third World misery, but it's not what it ought to be in a rich society, the richest in the world, in fact, with plenty of wealth around, which people can see, just not in their pockets.

All of this has now been brought to the fore. You can say that it's now almost a standard framework of discussion. Even the terminology is accepted. That's a big shift.

Earlier this month, the Pew Foundation released one of its annual polls surveying what people think is the greatest source of tension and conflict in American life. For the first time ever, concern over income inequality was way at the top. It's not that the poll measured income inequality itself, but the degree to which public recognition, comprehension and understanding of the issue has gone up. That's a tribute to the Occupy movement which put this strikingly critical fact of modern life on the agenda so that people who may have known of it from their own personal experience see that they are not alone, that this is all of us. In fact, the U.S. is off the spectrum on this. The inequalities have risen to historically unprecedented heights. In the words of the first lines of the report: "The Occupy Wall Street movement no longer occupies Wall Street, but the issue of class conflict has captured a growing share of the national consciousness. A new Pew Research Center survey of 2,048 adults finds that about two-thirds of the public (66%) believes there are 'very strong' or 'strong' conflicts between the rich and the poor—an increase of 19 percentage points since 2009. Not only have perceptions of class conflict grown more prevalent; so, too, has the belief that these disputes are intense."*

Meanwhile, coverage of the Occupy movement itself has been varied. In some places, for example, parts of the business press, there has been fairly sympathetic coverage occasionally. Of course, the general picture has been: "Why don't they go home and let us get on with our work?"

---

* Rich Morin, "Rising Share of Americans See Conflict Between Rich and Poor," Pew Research Center, January 11, 2012.

"Where is their political program?" "How do they fit into the mainstream structure of how things are supposed to change?" And so on.

And then came the repression, which of course was inevitable. It was pretty clearly coordinated across the country. Some of it was brutal, other places less so, and there's been kind of a stand-off. Some occupations have, in effect, been removed. Others have filtered back in some other form. Some of the things have been covered, like the use of pepper spray, and so on. But a lot of it, again, is just "why don't they go away and leave us alone?" That's to be anticipated.

The question of how to respond to it—the primary way is one of the points that you made: reaching out to bring into the general Occupation, in a metaphorical sense, to bring in much wider sectors of the population. There is a lot of sympathy for the goals and aims of the Occupy movement. They're quite high in polls, in fact. But that's a big step short from engaging people in it. It has to become part of their lives, something they think they can do something about. So it's necessary to get out to where people live. That means not just sending a message, but if possible, and it would be hard, to try to spread and deepen one of the real achievements of the movement which doesn't get discussed that much in the media—at least I haven't seen it. One of the main achievements has been to create communities, real functioning communities of mutual support, democratic interchange, care for one another, and so on. This is highly significant, especially in a society like ours in which people tend to be very isolated and neighborhoods are broken down, community structures have broken down, people are kind of alone.

There's an ideology that takes a lot of effort to implant: it's so inhuman that it's hard to get into people's heads, the ideology to just take care of yourself and forget about anyone else. An extreme version is the Ayn Rand version. Actually, there's been an effort for 150 years, literally, to try to impose that way of thinking on people.

During the onset of the Industrial Revolution in Eastern Massachusetts, mid-nineteenth century, there happened to be a very lively press run by working people, young women in the factories, artisans in the mills, and so on. They had their own press that was very interesting, very widely read and had a lot of support. And they bitterly condemned the way the industrial system was taking away their freedom and liberty and imposing on them rigid hierarchical structures that they didn't want. One of their main complaints was what they called "the new spirit of the age: gain wealth forgetting all but self." For 150 years there have been massive efforts to try to impose "the new spirit of the age" on people. But it's so inhuman that there's a lot of resistance, and it continues.

One of the real achievements of the Occupy movement, I think, has been to develop a real manifestation of rejection of this in a very striking way. The people involved are not in it for themselves. They're in it for one another, for the broader society and for future generations. The bonds and associations being formed, if they can persist and if they can be brought into the wider community, would be the real defense against the inevitable repression with its sometimes violent manifestations.

How best do you think the Occupy movement should go about engaging in these, what methods should be employed, and do you think it would be prudent to actually have space to decentralize bases of operation, at least within New York City, the five boroughs?

It would certainly make sense to have spaces, whether they should be open public spaces or not. To what extent they should be is a kind of a tactical decision that has to be made on the basis of a close evaluation of circumstances, the degree of support, the degree of opposition. They're different for different places, and I don't know of any general statement.

As for methods, people in this country have problems and concerns, and if they can be helped to feel that these problems and concerns are part of a broader movement of people who support them and who they support, well then it can take off. There is no single way of doing it. There is no one answer.

You might go into a neighborhood and find that their concerns may be as simple as a traffic light on the street where kids cross to go to school. Or maybe their concerns are to prevent people from being tossed out of their homes on foreclosures. Or maybe it's to try to develop community-based enterprises, which are not at all inconceivable— enterprises owned and managed by the work force and the community which can then overcome the choice of some remote multinational and board of directors made out of banks to shift production somewhere else. These are real, very live issues happening all the time. And it can be done. Actually, a lot of it is being done in scattered ways.

A whole range of other things can be done, like addressing police brutality and civic corruption. The reconstruction of media so that it comes right out of the communities, is perfectly possible. People can have a live media system that's community-based, ethnic-based, labor-based and other groupings. All of that can be done. It takes work and it can bring people together.

Actually, I've seen things done in various places that are models of what could be followed. I'll give you an example. I happened to be in Brazil a couple of years ago and I was spending some time with Lula, the former president of Brazil, but this was before he was elected president. He was a labor activist. We traveled around together. One day he took me out to a suburb of Rio. The suburbs of Brazil are where most of the poor people live. The rich people live downtown. The suburbs don't have very much, but there are millions of people.

They have semi-tropical weather there, and the evening Lula took me out there were a lot of people in the public square. Around 9:00 p.m., prime TV time, a small group of media professionals from the town had set up a truck in the middle of the square. Their truck had a TV screen above it that presented skits and plays written and acted by people in the community. Some of them were for fun, but others addressed serious issues like debt and AIDS. As people gathered in the square, the actors walked around with microphones asking people to comment on the material that had been presented. They were filmed commenting and were shown on the screen for other people to see it. People sitting in a small bar nearby or walking in the streets began reacting, and in no time you had interesting interchanges and discussions among people about quite serious topics, topics that are part of their lives.

Well, if it can be done in a poor Brazilian slum, we can certainly do it in many other places. I'm not suggesting we do just that, but these are the kinds of things that can be done to engage broader sectors and give people a reason to feel that they can be a part of the formation of communities and the development of serious programs adapted to whatever the serious needs happen to be.

From very simple things up to starting a new socio-economic system with worker and community-run enterprises, a whole range of things is possible. I don't think there's any particular formula to go about doing it any more than there has been in any other popular movement. With a little imagination, initiative and engagement, I think many such possibilities are opened up and that's a means of defense. The more active public support there is the better defense there is against repression and violence.

How would you go about dealing with the daunting task of getting money out of politics? And can you see that happening as an extension of the community involvement and engagement that you were just talking about?

Getting money out of politics is a very crucial matter; it has been for a long time. It's gotten much more extreme now. For a long time, elections have just been public relations extravaganzas where people are mobilized every four years to get excited to go push a button and then go home and forget about it. There are a lot of ways to go about overcoming that; some reach as far as organizing for constitutional conventions in order to take away corporate personhood. We're not anywhere near that. There are a bunch of more short-term things that are possible.

We happen to be in a primary period right now. The way primaries are carried out in the United States is radically undemocratic, and this is just taken for granted. Candidates show up to a town—lots of publicity, a lot of ads and so on. They then tell the people in the town, "Here's who I am, here's what I'm going to do." Of course they don't say much. And if they do say anything no one has a reason to believe them.

It's possible to imagine a primary that is done democratically. As I mentioned to Occupy Boston, the people in the town would get together, have town meetings and discussions and come up with some ideas about what they think ought to be done in the locality, in the country, foreign policy, the whole range. They might just pick their own candidates; or, if there are national candidates running, they could say, "You can come to visit us if you'd like, but we don't want to hear speeches from you. We're going to tell you what we think policy ought to be. And if you can convince us that you'll accept these policies and carry them forward, then maybe we'll vote for you." Either that or direct representation coming out of the communities would be a democratic alternative to the farcical system that we simply take for granted.

There are many other possibilities of getting money out of politics, broader ways that involve legislation and so on. These things are not in conflict with one another. There are lots of ways of going about the same ends and they are a very critical part. It's not just elections.

Things have reached a point in the United States where, even within Congress, if someone wants a position with a degree of power and authority, they literally have to buy it. It used to be that committee chairs were granted by a political party on the basis of seniority, service and other factors. Now, you literally have to pay the party to be a candidate for a chair. Well, that has an effect, too; it drives members of Congress into the same pockets if they want to get anywhere. Again, this is not 100 percent, but these are pretty widespread tendencies and are tending to fragment whatever is left of functioning democracy. You can see it in the campaigns that are just farcical.

Considering that the movement began with a relatively large dose of anarchist inspiration, how do you think we can best recapture the meaning of that term in society and dispel all the various stereotypes that exist?

To dispel the stereotypes you have to be doing something concrete and constructive that people can identify with. So, in fact, the spontaneous development of communities of mutual support and democratic participation is something that people can comprehend, and it can be considered to be a value for themselves which they can maybe develop in some other way in their own communities. That's the only way to get rid of stereotypes and develop your own conceptions of what a meaningful system of liberty and mutual aid would be like. You learn these things by doing them, and others will be brought in to the extent they see something valuable in it.

How do you assess the goals of the Democratic Party as far as co-opting the movement and what should we be vigilant and looking out for?

The Republican Party abandoned the pretense of being a political party years ago. They are committed, so uniformly and with such dedication, to tiny sectors of power and profit that they're hardly a political party any more. They have a catechism they have to repeat like a caricature of the old Communist Party. They have to do something to get a voting constituency. Of course, they can't get it from the 1 percent, to use the imagery, so they've been mobilizing sectors of the population that were always there, but not politically organized very well—religious evangelicals, nativists who are terrified that their rights and country are being taken away, and so on.

The Democrats are a little bit different and have different constituencies, but they're following pretty much the same path as the Republican Party. The centrist Democrats of today, the ones who essentially run the party, are pretty much the moderate Republicans of a generation ago and they are now kind of the mainstream of the Democratic Party. They are going to try to organize and mobilize—co-opt if you like—the constituency that's in their interest. They have pretty much abandoned the white working-class; it's rather striking to see. So that's barely part of their constituency at this point, which is a pretty sad development. They will try to mobilize Hispanics, Blacks and progressives. They'll try to reach out to the Occupy movement.

Organized labor is still part of the Democratic constituency and they'll try to co-opt them; and with Occupy, it's just the same as all the others. The political leadership will pat them on the head and say, "I'm for you, vote for me." The people involved will have to understand that maybe they'll do something for you, that only if you maintain substantial pressure can you get elected leadership to do things—but they're not going to do it on their own, with very rare exceptions.

As far as money and politics are concerned, it's hard to beat the comment of the great political financier, Mark Hanna. About a century ago, he was asked what was important in politics. He answered, "The first is money, the second one is money and I've forgotten what the third one is."

That was a century ago. Today it's much more extreme. So yes, concentrated wealth will, of course, try to use its wealth and power to take over the political system as much as possible, and to run it and do what it wants, etc. It would be a miracle if it didn't. The public has to find ways to struggle against that.

Centuries ago, political theorists like David Hume, in one of his foundations for government, pointed out correctly that power is in the hands of the governed and not the governors. This is true for a feudal society, a military state or a parliamentary democracy. Power is in the hands of the governed. The only way the rulers can overcome that is by control of opinions and attitudes.

Hume was right in the mid-eighteenth century. What he said remains true today. The power is in the hands of the general population. There are massive efforts to control it by less force today because of the many rights that have been won. Methods now are by propaganda, consumerism, stirring up ethnic hatred, all kinds of ways. Sure, that will always go on but we have to find ways to resist it.

There is nothing wrong with giving tentative support to a particular candidate as long as that person is doing what you want. But it would be a more democratic society if we could also recall them without a huge effort. There are other ways of pressuring candidates. There is a fine line between doing that and being co-opted, mobilized to serve someone else's interest. But those are just constant decisions and choices that have to be made.

Could you speak a little about Antonio Gramsci, how his ideas relate to the things you've been talking about.

I like Gramsci. He's an important person. He talked about things not unlike what David Hume was saying—how cultural hegemony was established by systems of power. I personally think that his work is worth reading. When I read it, it says much of what we already know. I don't find anything novel. Maybe it's just my inadequacy; you can read it and see what you think.

A great deal of our economics is dominated by the idea of more and more growth.

The whole human species currently faces a very serious problem of whether even decent existence can be carried forward. We are coming close to the edge of a precipice of environmental destruction. If growth is understood and accepted to include constant attacks on the physical environment that sustains life—like, for example, greenhouse emissions, destruction of agricultural land, and so forth—if that's what it means, then we are like lemmings walking over a cliff. This isn't what growth has to mean. For example, growth can mean simpler lives and more livable communities. It takes work and doesn't just come by itself. It takes labor and development of a different kind. Part of what functioning, free communities like the Occupy communities can be working for and spreading to others is just a different way of living, which is not based on maximizing consumer goods, but on maximizing values that are important for life. That's growth, too, just growth in a different direction.

Can you talk about the most recent crisis of the real estate bubble, how we got to this point in terms of historical context, why you think it occurred and what was at the root of its occurrence?

At the root of its occurrence is the major shift in the economy that began to take place in the 1970s. It was escalated radically under Reagan, Thatcher in England and on from there. There was a big growth period in the United States, the largest in history, during the 1950s and 1960s. At that time, there was also egalitarianism: the lowest quintile did as well as the highest quintile and it absorbed into the mainstream society. Groups that had been excluded from society, African Americans for example, could finally be integrated into society. That came to an end in the 1970s when, for one thing, there was a shift towards increasing the role of finance in the society.

One of the great financial correspondents, Martin Wolf, wrote recently that the financial systems are wiping out functioning markets the way larva destroys a host. He's one of the most respected financial economists in the world and not a radical. That's what the effect of the financial system has been. Combined with this were corporate decisions to ship production abroad. It's not a law of nature, again. You can have decent working conditions and production at home and abroad, but they made more profit that way. These decisions greatly changed the economy. One effect of this was that wealth became concentrated heavily in financial industries and that led to concentration of political power that leads to legislation, so on and so forth, keeping the vicious cycle going.

Part of this was deregulation. During the 1950s and 1960s, the great growth period, the banks were regulated and there was no crisis. No major bubbles burst. Starting in the 1980s, you started getting financial crises, bubbles. There were several during the Reagan administrations. The Clinton administration ended with a huge tech-bubble burst.

There is a lot of money floating around, and much less real production that people need. One of the ways in which households were able to survive during the period of stagnation was just by getting caught up in bubbles. Early in this century, housing prices started to shoot up way beyond the trend. There is a kind of trend line for about a century. Housing prices roughly match gross domestic product. About ten years ago, they just started shooting way out of sight, with no fundamentals. A lot of it was essentially robbery: subprime mortgages and complicated devices by which the banks could slice up mortgages so that others would have responsibility when it collapsed, complicated derivatives and other financial instruments. All of this took off and created a huge bubble that was obviously going to burst. It was barely even noticed by the entire economist profession, including the Federal Reserve.

The minutes of the 2006 Federal Reserve

meeting came out recently, you might have seen them. And rather strikingly, there was no recognition there that there was a multi-trillion dollar housing bubble that had no basis whatsoever and was going to collapse. As a matter of fact, they were congratulating themselves on how marvelously they were running the economy. Well, of course, it collapsed as it had to, maybe 8 trillion dollars lost.

For much of the population, that's all they had. Many African Americans' net worth was practically reduced to nothing, and many others, too. It's a disaster. This kind of thing is going to happen as long as you have unregulated capital markets, which furthermore have a government insurance policy. It's called "too big to fail": if you get in trouble, the taxpayer will bail you out—policies that, of course, lead to underestimation of risk.

Credit agencies already take into account the fact that it's going to be rescued next time it goes bust. Well, that of course increases risk even further. If not housing, it'll be something else, commodities or whatever.

It's a financial casino instead of a protected economy, and of course people get hurt who are not rich and powerful, the 99 percent.

Shopping
2ND TIME IVE
FOUGHT FOR
MY COUNTRY
1ST TIME
IVE KNOWN
MY ENEMY

OCCUPYING FOREIGN POLICY

University of Maryland Friday, January 27, 2012

How do we occupy the foreign-policy establishment?

The same way you bring about other changes. By comparative standards, the United States remains a very free country. You get a lot of opportunities. They range from electoral politics to demonstrations, resistance and organizing public pressure. That's the way you do it.

In fact, you don't have to go very far. The educational establishment, the intellectual establishment, is up to their neck in this. And we live right in the middle of it. Of course, that can be influenced, you know, in classrooms and writing and organization and all sorts of things.

I hear the question often and I don't really understand it. In the United States we can do almost anything we want. It's not like Egypt, where you're going to get murdered by the security forces. Here, there's some repression sometimes: but by international standards, by comparative standards, it's so slight that it hardly counts, certainly for privileged people—not for poor people. They can get it in the neck. But for those with privilege, the opportunities are just overwhelming. There's nothing to stop all kinds of action, from education and organizing to political action, to demonstrations. All kinds of resistance are possible, the kinds of things that have succeeded in the past.

After all, we have a history of success in getting policy changes. The New Deal legislation, for example, didn't come out of nowhere. That came out of very large-scale popular activism, which reached the point where the business world and the government agreed to allow progressive legislation to pass. The business world quickly tried to undermine it, but they had to accept it. By the time sit-down strikes were taking place, the business world could easily see that the next step is just taking over the factory, running it, and kicking them out. Well, they didn't want to allow that, so some legislation, important legislation passed. And under other massive popular organization and pressure, other things happened.

Similar things have happened since. In the 1960s, for example, the antiwar movement, which I mentioned, it got from essentially nowhere to a strong mass popular movement by 1968. If you read the Pentagon Papers, one of the most interesting sections is the final section, which ends in mid-1968. If you take a look at that section, you'll see that during the first few months of 1968, the president wanted to send hundreds of thousands more troops to South Vietnam. The military and the Joint Chiefs were opposed because they said that they would need the troops for civil disorder control in the United States. The population was just going to get out of control—young people, women, minorities, others. They knew that they would need the troops to control the population here so they didn't send them. Well, you know, when the government gets that wary, you've had an effect. They did other horrible things—clandestine things that could've been worse, but it was bad enough, like I mentioned.

Actually, the same thing happened in the Iraq War. The protests against the Iraq War were historically totally unique. I think it's the first war in history where there was massive protest before the war was officially launched. I can't think of a case where that ever happened. And it's claimed that the protests had no effect, but I don't think that's true. It should have gone on. Unfortunately, it reduced, and that allowed more leeway for aggression.

But the Iraq War was nothing like the war against South Vietnam. The policies that Kennedy and Johnson routinely carried out without even thinking about it were never tried in Iraq. There was no chemical warfare, there was no saturation bombing by B-52s, there was no—what are called "population control measures"—where you drive the population into concentration camps. None of those measures were even tried. And I think one reason they weren't tried was because it was understood that the public was not going to tolerate them this time. So, okay, it had a kind of a retarding effect.

There are other kinds of popular organization that have had major effects. The country is a much more civilized place now than it was in the 1960s in many respects. Take, for example, women's rights. In the 1960s, women literally still were not guaranteed the right to serve on juries. They'd won the right to vote forty years before, but by the 1960s, in many states, they couldn't serve on juries. In 1960, my university was almost 100 percent white male. Now it's much more diverse and that's the case over much of the country.

Well, that's a big change in the nature of the society and the culture. It didn't happen by magic. It wasn't a gift from above. It came from extensive organizing activities and corresponding actions which finally broke down a lot of barriers and freed things up. That's the way changes take place. And all those methods are still available.

I was wondering if you have read Gar Alperovitz's

book America Beyond Capitalism, *and if you have, what you thought of his ideas in the book.*

It's a very important book, and the work that's described there is extremely important. The book reviews work that Alperovitz has been involved in for some years in trying to develop worker-owned enterprises, mostly in Ohio. That's one of the things that can be done. It's very feasible.

Actually, if you could take a look at standard texts in business economics—you know, nothing radical—standard texts in business economics point out that there's no economic principle or any other principle that says that *shareholders* should have a higher priority than *stakeholders*— workers and community. Shareholders, incidentally, doesn't mean somebody whose pension fund has two dollars as a share. Shareholders are very narrowly concentrated, the top 1 percent of the population, and that means big banks, interlocking directorates, and so on. There's no economic principle that says they are the ones who should determine investment policy, like shipping production to Foxconn. There's no law of economics that says that has to happen. It could just as well be done by stakeholders, by the workforce and the community—perfectly consistent with anything that anyone claims about economic theory.

There's no reason for the Occupy movement to be less imaginative and ambitious than standard business texts. So, yes, stakeholders could take over parts of the economy that are being dismantled, run them effectively, and direct them to different purposes. These are very feasible tasks.

So, for example, one of the things that Obama is praised for by left-liberal economists, Paul Krugman and others, is for having essentially nationalized the auto industry and reconstructed it. That's pretty much what happened. Well, once the auto industry was nationalized, there were alternatives. And one alternative was to reconstruct it and hand it back to the original owners—not to the same names, but to the same class, the same banks, and so on. That's what was done. Another possibility would have been to hand the auto industry over to the workforce and the communities, the stakeholders, and redirect it towards things that the country really needs.

These are the kinds of things that Gar Alperovitz is talking about, feasible things that could have a big effect on the society. And Alperovitz is one of the very few people who is really doing very good work on this. His book is certainly worth reading and thinking about what it describes and what options it suggests.

Examples come up all the time. Here's one from a place near where I live. About a year ago in Taunton, a manufacturing town outside of Boston, there was a small, reasonably successful manufacturing plant. It was producing high-tech equipment for aircraft, and it apparently was doing okay; but it wasn't making enough profit for the managers and the multinational corporation that owned it. So the corporation wanted to just dismantle it. The United Electrical Workers Union wanted to buy the operation and run it themselves, but the corporation wouldn't agree. I suspect that it wouldn't agree mostly on class grounds: it's not a good idea to let people own and manage their own workplaces—people might get the wrong idea. Anyhow, whatever the reason, it didn't work.

But if the Occupy movement had been around back then and had been active and energetic enough and had reached out sufficiently, that's the kind of thing it could have participated in and supported; and maybe it could have helped the workers gain the edge they needed to win. These are the kinds of options that are all over the place right now, ones that support from a movement can really impact.

AUDIENCE: Can we get a question from a woman?

M.C.: Fair enough. Thank you—.

WOMAN FROM THE AUDIENCE: I am an adjunct professor, what's known as a "Beltway adjunct." I teach eight classes a semester, and I have no health insurance and no retirement benefits. I'm a communications scholar, and I've studied your work for the last fifteen years. And I want to know, beyond the critique—which was a marvelous critique, by the way, thank you—what are the discursive strategies that we can use to combat the ideologically driven discourse that dominates the politics that we deal with in the classroom and beyond every day? I know I have friends, colleagues, and family members who are staunch supporters of the Republican worldview, and it's hard to have meaningful dialogues with them. Facts no longer seem to matter. That being the case, how do we begin to talk about truth in a meaningful way? What kind of linguistic strategies do we use to drive change?

Just about every talk I give, the same question comes up: how about allowing a question from a woman? Why does that question even arise? We don't ask the question, "How about allowing a question from somebody with blonde hair?" Why is the discrimination so deeply embedded, and in fact internalized, that we still have to raise the question? And it's uniform. I can't remember a talk where this didn't come up. So that's something to think about. That's still a battle to be won internally and in the society.

As far as the discursive strategies are concerned, I don't think there are any answers other than the ones we all know, the ones that have succeeded—not 100 percent, of course. Every success is limited. There are failures. But there are successes.

There are things practically everybody can do, and if you are from a privileged sector of the population, then there are even more opportunities. You can speak, you can write, you can organize, you can reach out to other people. If you keep doing it, it can have an impact.

Take a case like the women's movement. I mean, a lot of you are old enough to remember how that happened. It began with very small consciousness-raising groups—groups of women getting together and talking to each other and coming to identify and comprehend that, first of all there is oppression, and that a better way is possible where we don't have to accept oppression. If you had asked my grandmother if she was oppressed, she wouldn't have known what you were talking about. Of course, she was hopelessly oppressed, but identifying it is not always easy, especially if no one talks about it. So just getting to understand that you don't have to accept oppression, that you can be a free and independent person, is a big step. The women's movement took that step and kept going. There was bitter resistance; it wasn't easy by any means. And, in fact, there still is, and there's a backlash, and so on and so forth. But you just keep struggling for it.

The civil rights movement didn't get anywhere near Martin Luther King's dream, but it did bring big change. Things are still bad, but not like they were in Alabama in 1960. The organizing goes back decades, of course, but it really took off when a couple of young black students sat in at a lunch counter about sixty-one years ago. Pretty soon, the SNCC formed, the Student Nonviolent Coordinating Committee. The students got some support in Spelman College in Atlanta, where a lot of the SNCC activists came from. There were two faculty members who supported them— Howard Zinn and Staughton Lynd—and both got expelled. But they did get some support. And the Freedom Riders' bus trips started. There was a little participation from the North.

Repression against the movement was very brutal. People were beaten and killed. You know, not fun. I mean, I remember demonstrations in 1965, in the South, where the police violence was brutal and federal marshals stood around, kind of watching them, not doing anything.

Things hit a limit as soon as they reached the North. It's striking. In 1966, Martin Luther King expanded the movement to Chicago; then they were just dumped on miserably. It was an effort to mobilize people, starting with the poor, around the issue of slums. When they moved on to criticize the war in Vietnam, there was huge antagonism against them. They ended up the way I described, mostly written out of history by Northern liberals. But they did have successes, and the successes are real, and we know how they were won.

Same with everything else. For example, the Vietnam War protests did reach a substantial level, but remember what it was like for years. When I started giving talks about the Vietnam War in the early 1960s, they were usually held in somebody's living room or in a church with four or five people attending. And in fact, if we tried to do it at the college, MIT, you'd have to bring together half a dozen topics and make one of them Vietnam in the hope that somebody would show up. As late as October 1965 in Boston, which is a liberal city, you could not have a public demonstration against the war, literally. It would be violently broken up, often by students. It's a fact.

By March 1966, there were hundreds of thousands of U.S. troops rampaging in South Vietnam, destroying huge parts of the country. Since we couldn't have public demonstrations in Boston without their getting broken up, we tried to have one in a church downtown. As a result of our event, the church was attacked, defaced with tomatoes and cans. A police contingent was sent. I walked outside and stood next to the police captain and asked him, "Can't you do something to stop the defacing of the church?" And he said, no, he couldn't do anything. A moment later, a tomato hit him in the face, and in about thirty seconds the place was cleared. A year later, there were big demonstrations.

And there were no special strategies or tricks leading up to the demonstrations, just what we all know how to do. If people don't want to think about what's going on, try to bring up the importance of understanding facts. In fact, if you look at public attitudes, even Tea Party attitudes, they're kind of social-democratic, literally. So, for example, among Tea Party advocates and, of course, the rest of the population, a considerable majority are in favor of more spending for health and more spending for education. They're against welfare, but more spending to help, say, women with dependent children.

That's the result of very effective propaganda. One of Ronald Reagan's great successes was to demonize the concept of welfare. In Reaganite rhetoric, welfare means a rich black woman driving to a welfare office in a chauffeured Cadillac so she can take your hard-earned money and spend it on drugs or something. Well, nobody's in favor of that. But are you in favor of what welfare actually does? Yeah, that ought to supported.

The same is true on health, on the deficit and the other things I mentioned. I think it's two-thirds of the population that thinks that corporations should be deprived of personal rights. If that were to be enacted, it would be a pretty significant move. It would undo a century of court decisions. It's not just Citizens United. It goes back a century. And that's against the will of about two-thirds of the population. Well, all these things offer plenty of opportunities for discussion, interchange, education, organizing and activism. The opportunities are all there.

WE ARE CITIZENS. We must not put ourselves in the position of looking at the world from [politicians'] eyes and say, "Well, we have to compromise, we have to do this for political reasons." No, we have to speak our minds.

This is the position that the abolitionists were in before the Civil War, and people said, "Well, you have to look at it from Lincoln's point of view." Lincoln didn't believe that his first priority was abolishing slavery. But the anti-slavery movement did, and the abolitionists said, "We're not going to put ourselves in Lincoln's position. We are going to express our own position, and we are going to express it so powerfully that Lincoln will have to listen to us."

And the anti-slavery movement grew large enough and powerful enough that Lincoln had to listen. That's how we got the Emancipation Proclamation and the Thirteenth and Fourteenth and Fifteenth Amendments.

That's been the story of this country. Where progress has been made, wherever any kind of injustice has been overturned, it's been because people acted as citizens, and not as politicians. They didn't just moan. They worked, they acted, they organized, they rioted if necessary to bring their situation to the attention of people in power. And that's what we have to do today.*

—HOWARD ZINN

* Howard Zinn, "Changing Obama's Mindset," *The Progressive*, May 2009. Accessed August 18, 2013: http://progressive.org/zinn0509.html.

REMEMBERING HOWARD ZINN

It is not easy for me to write a few words about Howard Zinn, the great American activist and historian. He was a very close friend for forty-five years. The families were very close, too. His wife, Roz, who died of cancer not long before, was also a marvelous person and close friend. Also somber is the realization that a whole generation seems to be disappearing, including several other old friends: Edward Said, Eqbal Ahmed and others, who were not only astute and productive scholars, but also dedicated and courageous militants, always on call when needed—which was constant. A combination that is essential if there is to be hope of decent survival.

Howard's remarkable life and work are summarized best in his own words. His primary concern, he explained, was "the countless small actions of unknown people" that lie at the roots of "those great moments" that enter the historical record—a record that will be profoundly misleading, and seriously disempowering, if it is torn from these roots as it passes through the filters of doctrine and dogma. His life was always closely intertwined with his writings and innumerable talks and interviews. It was devoted, selflessly, to empowerment of the unknown people who brought about great moments. That was true when he was an industrial worker and labor activist, and from the days, fifty years ago, when he was teaching at Spelman College in Atlanta, Georgia, a black college that was open mostly to the small black elite.

While teaching at Spelman, Howard supported the students who were at the cutting edge of the civil rights movement in its early and most dangerous days, many of whom became quite well-known in later years—Alice Walker, Julian Bond and others—and who loved and revered him, as did everyone who knew him well. And as always, he did not just support them, which was rare enough, but also participated directly with them in their most hazardous efforts—no easy undertaking at that time, before there was any organized popular movement and in the face of government hostility that lasted for some years. Finally, popular support was ignited, in large part by the courageous actions of the young people who were sitting in at lunch counters, riding freedom buses, organizing demonstrations, facing bitter racism and brutality, sometimes death.

By the early 1960s, a mass popular movement was taking shape, by then with Martin Luther King in a leadership role—and the government had to respond. As a reward for his courage and honesty, Howard was soon expelled from the college where he taught. A few years later, he wrote the standard work on SNCC (the Student Non-violent Coordinating Committee), the major organization of those "unknown people" whose "countless small actions" played such an important part in creating the groundswell that enabled King to gain significant influence—as I am sure he would have been the first to say—and to bring the country to honor the constitutional amendments of a century earlier that had theoretically granted elementary civil rights to former slaves— at least to do so partially; no need to stress that there remains a long way to go.

A Civilizing Influence

On a personal note, I came to know Howard well when we went together to a civil rights demonstration in Jackson Mississippi in (I think) 1964, even at that late date, a scene of violent public antagonism, police brutality and indifference—or even cooperation—with state security forces on the part of federal authorities, sometimes in ways that were quite shocking. After being expelled from the

Atlanta college where he taught, Howard came to Boston, and spent the rest of his academic career at Boston University, where he was, I am sure, the most admired and loved faculty member on campus, and the target of bitter antagonism and petty cruelty on the part of the administration. In later years, however, after his retirement, he gained the public honor and respect that was always overwhelming among students, staff, much of the faculty, and the general community. While there, Howard wrote the books that brought him well-deserved fame. His book *Logic of Withdrawal*, in 1967, was the first to express clearly and powerfully what many were then beginning barely to contemplate: that the United States had no right even to call for a negotiated settlement in Vietnam, leaving Washington with power and substantial control in the country it had invaded and had by then already largely destroyed.

Rather, the United States should do what any aggressor should: withdraw; allow the population to somehow reconstruct as they could from the wreckage; and, if minimal honesty could be attained, pay massive reparations for the crimes that the invading armies had committed, vast crimes in this case. The book had wide influence among the public, although to this day, its message can barely even be comprehended in elite educated circles, an indication of how much necessary work lies ahead. Significantly, among the general public by the war's end, 70 per cent regarded the war as "fundamentally wrong and immoral," not "a mistake," a remarkable figure, considering the fact that scarcely a hint of such a thought was expressible in mainstream opinion. Howard's writings—and, as always, his prominent presence in protest and direct resistance—were a major factor in civilizing much of the country.

In those same years, Howard also became one of the most prominent supporters of the resistance movement that was then developing. He was one of the early signers of the Call to Resist Illegitimate Authority and was so close to the activities of Resist that he was practically one of the organizers. He also took part at once in the sanctuary actions that had a remarkable impact in galvanizing anti-war protest. Whatever was needed—talks, participation in civil disobedience, support for resisters, testimony at trials—Howard was always there.

History from Below

Even more influential in the long run than Howard's anti-war writings and actions was his enduring masterpiece, *A People's History of the United States*, a book that literally changed the consciousness of a generation. Here he developed with care, lucidity and comprehensive sweep his fundamental message about the crucial role of the people who remain unknown in carrying forward the endless struggle for peace and justice, and about the victims of the systems of power that create their own versions of history and seek to impose it. Later, his *Voices of the People's History*, now an acclaimed theatrical and television production, brought to many the actual words of those forgotten or ignored people who have played such a valuable role in creating a better world.

Howard's unique success in drawing the actions and voices of unknown people from the depths to which they had largely been consigned has spawned extensive historical research following a similar path, focusing on critical periods of U.S. history, and turning to the record in other countries as well, a very welcome development. It is not entirely novel—there had been scholarly inquiries of particular topics before—but nothing to compare with Howard's broad and incisive evocation of "history from below," compensating for critical omissions in how U.S. history had been interpreted and conveyed. Howard's dedicated activism continued, literally without a break, until the very end, even in his last years, when he was suffering from severe infirmity and personal loss—though one would hardly know it when meeting him or watching him speaking tirelessly to captivated audiences all over the country. Whenever there was a struggle for peace and justice, Howard was there, on the front lines, unflagging in his enthusiasm, and inspiring in his integrity, engagement, eloquence and insight; a light touch of humor in the face of adversity; and dedication to non-violence and sheer decency. It is hard even to imagine how many young people's lives were touched, and how deeply, by his achievements, both in his work and his life. There are places where Howard's life and work should have particular resonance. One, which should be much better known, is Turkey. I know of no other country where leading writers, artists, journalists, academics and other intellectuals have compiled such an impressive record of bravery and integrity in condemning crimes of the state, and going beyond to engage in civil disobedience to try to bring oppression and violence to an end, facing and sometimes enduring severe repression, and then returning to the task.

It is an honorable record, unique to my knowledge, a record of which the country should be proud. And one that should be a model for others, just as Howard Zinn's life and work are an unforgettable model, sure to leave a permanent stamp on how history is understood and how a decent and honorable life should be lived.

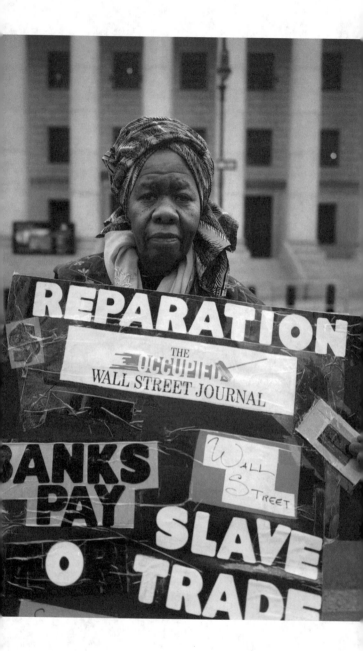

THERE'S NOTHING LIKE DIRECT INTERACTION

Excerpts from Air Occupy interview with Noam Chomsky

December 11, 2012

In your book Media Control, *you say, "Propaganda is to democracy what the bludgeon is to a totalitarian state." I know that is an oft-quoted passage, but I don't think that, by and large, Americans really understand that we're being fed propaganda.*

There are various kinds of propaganda systems. There's the kind that they had in Russia in the old days, which was overt. The government said, *here's what you are supposed to believe.* Okay, so maybe people would accept it, maybe not, but they had no doubt as to where it was coming from. A sophisticated propaganda system won't do that. It won't state the doctrines you are supposed to believe. It will just presuppose them, so they become like the air you breathe. That's the basis for discussion. Then we have debate within those limits.

Take domestic affairs. The big issue is: What

do we do about the deficit? It's a huge problem in the political system, in Washington, in the media. What do we do about the deficit? And then you have various suggestions about what to do. Take a look at public opinion. Public opinion does not regard the deficit as a major problem. The people regard joblessness as the problem, and they are right. The deficit is not a major problem, but the deficit is important to the banks and the other financial institutions. They are very powerful, so therefore we only discuss the deficit.

Take foreign affairs. The Middle East is a really critical issue. If you listened to the last presidential debate, you are a masochist. [Laughs] You noticed that one issue came up over and over: The greatest threat to world peace is Iran's nuclear program. That gets repeated in the political system and in the press—it's just taken for granted. It's as obvious as when the sun rises in the morning. Well, there are a couple of questions to ask about that, if you can extricate yourself from the doctrinal system. First of all, who thinks so? It turns out it's a Western obsession. People in the Arab world don't think so. In fact, they don't regard Iran as much of a threat. They regard the United States and Israel as the main threats. The nonaligned countries—that's most of the world—they don't think so. The Indians and so on don't regard Iran as a major threat. It's the United States and its allies. Second question is: Let's admit that it's a threat. If you believe it is, how could you deal with it? Well, there's a very simple way of dealing with it. You could move toward establishing a nuclear-weapons-free zone in the region, with inspections and so on. That's quite feasible. In fact, that can be done at this moment. Right now, there's supposed to be an international conference in Finland to carry forward this proposal, which is supported by almost the entire world.

Almost nobody knows about recent events that took place in the last few weeks, because they weren't reported. In early November, Iran said it would attend the conference. Israel had already indicated it wouldn't attend the conference. Immediately after Iran said it would attend the conference, Obama cancelled the conference. Immediately after that, the Arab states and the nonaligned movement pressed again to re-institute the conference. Nothing happening; it won't happen. Shortly after that, the United States carried out a nuclear-weapons test, which was protested. That's what's going on before our eyes, and that's the simple way to deal with whatever anyone thinks the threat is. I don't know if you would call that propaganda, but it is very effective subordination to power on the part of the educated community and the media system.

*Talking about media . . . Occupy does a lot of live
streaming, and I was wondering if you think this and
social media have democratized some of the media,
or do you think that it has made it more disparate, or
harder to get a clear picture because it's coming from
so many different sources?*

Social media have been very valuable. As you
say, Occupy uses them. In Egypt, the protesters
relied on them, and most activist movements
use them for almost everything: information,
announcements, organization. And they do allow
people to say things freely that, in some cases,
they would have no other way of saying. But on
the other hand, they don't compensate for a lack
of free, independent, major media. You and I
could have a Twitter account, but we can't have
correspondents in the Middle East. We can reach
scattered and selected sectors of the population, but not most people. So it's useful, and it
has very many positive effects. It also has some
very negative effects. I can just tell from mail I
receive. I receive a ton of email, hundreds a day,
and I try to answer. But an assistant pointed out
to me recently that a lot of the letters are getting
very short. In fact, she pointed out to me that a
lot of them are basically Twitter messages. Well,
what does that mean? That means that somebody
is walking on the street, and a thought comes to

your mind. Instead of thinking about it, you write a message to somebody and ask them to answer it. It becomes very superficial.

Dumbed down, in a way.

I don't happen to use a lot of social media. I'm old-fashioned and conservative in this area. But the impression that I get is that it sort of has an effect of trivializing relationships among people. It keeps them pretty superficial. And it has to, because of the nature of the medium. Now that doesn't mean we shouldn't use them. In fact, I think that they are very valuable. We should recognize them for what they are. They don't substitute for face-to-face contact, for a serious interaction, and for major media. In fact, one of the main contributions of Occupy, I thought, was that it brought people together in face-to-face contact. People were actually working together to do something in common, with mutual support, with solidarity, and that's something that's pretty much missing in this society. In fact, very much missing. And there's nothing like direct interaction—community interaction, not just two individuals—to carry forward these central things.

Since it began, the Occupy movement has continued to evolve. We've had things like Occupy [Hurricane]

Sandy, the Debt Strike and Rolling Jubilee, and a lot of foreclosure defense actions from Occupy Our Homes, especially in Atlanta and Minnesota, but also, all over the United States, there have also been a lot of conversations that are going on in hubs like Interoccupy.net. It feels to me like it is—and has been—an organic community action. Could you speak to the newest developments?

The Occupy movement began last September, a year ago. It was a brilliant tactic. I was surprised. Frankly, I would never have guessed that it would have worked. But I was wrong; it worked very well. But tactics are tactics. They have a kind of half-life. They don't go on, and you can't use them forever. They lose their efficacy. They just don't achieve anything after a certain point. Even just the actual "occupy" tactic couldn't really be carried on for very long—like, in most places, you couldn't carry it on over the winter. It's just impossible. So, I think a move had to be made, and by last winter, it was beginning to be made, towards diversifying the activities, reaching out beyond the kind of people who were able to sit in Zuccotti Park, or Dewey Square, or wherever, to communities, to other sectors of the population, and trying actually to engage the "99 percent" in activities and long-term programs. And the kind of things you've mentioned are steps in that direction, very healthy steps. I think that's the way the movement ought to be developing.

You can never predict where a popular movement is going and how it's going to succeed. That has never been possible. It's not possible now, and you couldn't have predicted that for the civil rights movement, the anti-war movement, the women's movement, anything. But this one has been pretty successful, I think. In fact, surprisingly so, to me. And it has a lot of potential, but I think it is going to have to go in the kinds of directions you mentioned—also, spreading out into neighborhoods.

There were these Occupy the Hood efforts, which I don't know how far they've gone, but I thought they were a very good idea. There was at one point an Occupy the Dream movement. That was an interesting one that brought together Occupy activists and activists from the old civil rights movement. The dream that they were talking about comes out of the civil rights movement. It's not the dream that we hear about on Martin Luther King Day, his "I Have a Dream" speech in 1963, but his actual dream that he worked on until the end of his life, and that he expressed again in a very eloquent speech just before he was assassinated—the dream that there would be a general movement of the poor. He called it a human rights movement: a movement of the poor for the things that people have a need and a right to—like housing, and food, and decent jobs, and so on. That's the dream. And Occupy the Dream was a way of bringing together the civil rights movement—which achieved a lot, but then was aborted as soon as it began to turn to class issues—a way of reviving that, and linking it up with the Occupy movements and many others that have developed in recent years. That could be a major popular movement. Occupy the Dream was a good slogan, but it has to be implemented. There are lots of other things that are very important, like the things you mentioned: anti-foreclosure, the Sandy rehabilitation, and so on.

I wonder if you might speak a little bit more about the need to build coalitions like that. I've always viewed Occupy as sort of a cathartic reaction to the financial circumstances, and viewed it as sort of an umbrella of lots of different grievances that people had and how we've linked those up. I think there were some orthodoxies at some of the camps—that people were afraid that OWS would be co-opted and the ideology of OWS, whatever that was at the time, was going to be spoiled somehow by including other groups, progressive groups.

You know, this is not a membership movement, so I don't know what it means, exactly, to include or exclude other groups. If people want to participate, great. They may participate with the same kind of general goals but with specific interests. For example, should you include anti-foreclosure movements? Yeah, I think you should, even though they are not the same as the effort to institute a financial transaction tax, which would be very important for dealing with fiscal problems. But it doesn't get anywhere, because the banks don't like it. Crucially, and here I agree with you totally, it has to include the labor movement. Unless the labor movement is revitalized the way it was in the 1930s, it's very unlikely that there will be a really mass popular movement that will be successful. Right now, the labor movement is under severe attack.

Actually, you see this elsewhere, too. In Egypt, for example, it is not talked about much, but a core participant in the Tahrir Square demonstrations—and other uprisings—a core participant is the labor movement that has been a very militant force for a long time. And when it joined and began to participate, it really began a mass movement. That's what's happened in the past in our own history. It happened in the 1930s. It happened in the late 1800s. The United States happens to have a very violent and repressive labor history, much more so than other industrial countries. There have been several very large,

militant popular movements based on labor—
and in earlier years, on farmers. The biggest popular, democratic, radical movement in American
history was the Populist movement based on
the Farmers' Alliance and the Knights of Labor,
a huge labor movement. The Farmers' Alliance
was based in Texas, which was the center of radical agrarian activism. Shows you how the world
has changed. That alliance was divided by racial
strategies and crushed by force. The labor movement was virtually dead in the 1920s, but revived
significantly in the 1930s. That's the main force
that led to the New Deal legislation and the fairly
successful economic development period in the
1950s and 1960s. That was also the background
for the achievements of the 1960s. That's been
under severe attack, and the Occupy movement
ought to be working really hard to link up with it.
Those are collaborations that I think are going to
have to be crucial.

LESSONS FROM OCCUPY SANDY AND BEYOND

Interview with *The Occupied Times of London*

February 2013

Since 2008, the latest crisis of capitalism has given birth to a new wave of horizontal and collective forms of organizing in the United States: the occupation of the State Capitol of Wisconsin in early 2011 in opposition to Governor Scott Walker's plan to drastically reduce collective-bargaining rights; the Occupy movement and its notorious occupation of Zuccotti Park in late 2011, followed by similar occupations of public space across hundreds of American cities; and, most recently, the network of relief hubs, organized at a community level and aimed at cultivating an atmosphere of mutual aid in the aftermath of Hurricane Sandy. Indeed, Occupy Sandy has been at the forefront of filling the gaps where the state seems absent. The last few months has witnessed the development of tools for debt resistance, exemplified by numerous debtors' assemblies held in city squares across America, and more recently, by the Rolling Jubilee, which aimed to display the power of collective refusal of debt peonage.

One unifying thread that runs through these recent

HOW DARE THEY
CALL US DIRTY!
WHAT HAVE THEY
DONE TO OUR
WATER, AIR, FOOD?
TITAN

and varied forms of collective organization is the lack of institutionalization. In fact, institutionalized forms of collective bargaining have been declining for some time. Today, U.S. union membership is lower than at any other time since 1933. Losses in private and public sector unions saw total union density fall from 11.8 percent to 11.3 percent last year. Meanwhile, anti-union laws are being pushed through state legislatures, most recently in Michigan.

After Hurricane Sandy, New York City seemed to turn into an authoritative vacuum. Nobody expected much help from the feds. Do you think that Occupy Sandy can capitalize on that feeling?

The trouble is, it is a double-edged sword, because to the extent that Occupy Sandy or other citizens' efforts are effective, they reduce the pressure on the federal government to stand up and do what it is supposed to do. That is a trap you want to be able to avoid. There also ought to be pressure on the feds to say: "You guys are supposed to be doing this."

So, Occupy Sandy and these various movements that have come out in the last year, they are double-edged in the sense that they are alleviating the pressure we should put on [governments], but they are also desired responses in many ways.

What ways? The trouble with saying "the government backs off" is that it only feeds the libertarians. The wealthy and the corporate sector are delighted to have government back off, because then they get more power. Suppose you were to develop a voluntary system, a community type, a mutual support system that takes care of social security—the wealthy sectors would be delighted.

Absolutely, so it's an interesting dilemma. The idea of mutual aid is very prevalent within Occupy Sandy. Because of the failure of government responses, it has resulted in this thing that can potentially be used against us in lots of ways.

It's difficult. In principle you are doing what a lot of communities ought to be doing. An organized community is just a government—in a democratic society at least, thus not in ours. The problem is the effectiveness of the whole doctrinal system that has undermined any belief in democracy. You see it on the front page of every newspaper. Why is there a fuss now about raising taxes? In a democratic society, you would have the opposite pressure to raise taxes, because you appreciate taxes; taxes are what we use to pay for the things we decide to do. But if the government is a big alien force, we don't want them to steal our money, so we're against taxes.

The idea of taxation seems so thoroughly demonized, even though it obviously results in things that everybody takes for granted.

I think the demonization is a consequence of the feeling that the government is not simply all of us formulating and carrying out our plans. If that's what the government was, people wouldn't object to taxes.

There's a lot of spillover from that sentiment—taxation and its implications for the average individual—to what we are seeing in terms of attacks on labor unions, like what just happened in Michigan.

It's been going on for 150 years, and it's a very business-driven society today. In almost every society business hates labor, but the United States is run by businesses to an unusual degree. It has a very violent labor history. Several times in the last century, labor has been practically destroyed, just through violence—government violence, business violence. Strikers were being murdered in the United States in the late 1930s, and in other countries for decades.

Many legal instruments have been used to discipline the labor force across the United States over the past few decades. One of the most damaging forms of legislation is known as Right to Work law. It exists on the statute books of nearly half of American states, primarily in the South. Its main function is to prohibit the requirement that workers pay union fees as a condition of employment. This doesn't prevent those who do not pay union membership fees from receiving the benefits of collective bargaining. The long-term effects of the legislation, as with most laws designed to restrict labor rights, is a lowering of wages and a worsening of safety and health conditions for workers. Regions that utilize these laws are often dismissively referred to as "right to work for less" states by their opponents.

What do you think of Michigan's legalization of collective bargaining or in-shop organizing? Did the integration of potentially radical tactics from the labor force take the ground away from under it? Or have they been normalized?

It just depends how it works. Legalizing collective bargaining made it possible to develop labor unions, but it really depends on how they work. Take the United States and Canada. They are pretty similar societies, but organized labor has worked in quite different ways. So the Americans got a good contract, a reasonably good contract for UAW workers, but nobody else did, and so we end up with this monstrosity.

Furthermore, the people in the UAW leadership weren't just thugs—they were seriously and unbelievably naive. They thought they could make a compact with management and work together. But by 1979, the head of the UAW, Doug Fraser, gave an important speech that is probably on the Internet. He pulled out of some labor-management group that the Carter administration was setting up, realizing it was a farce. He said that he realized a little late that business was fighting a one-sided class war against working people, that they don't mean it when they sign these contracts, and that they are just waiting for a chance to cut back and get out of them. And he said that he had finally figured out what workers knew 150 years ago: Business is fighting a bitter class war, all the time. The business world is full of dedicated, vulgar Marxists who are always fighting a class war, and the labor leadership didn't understand it, or wanted not to understand it. In any event, they entered into these compacts. Business wanted to undercut them, and they did, which is what is happening. Unions were demonized by massive propaganda—movies, advertising, everything. It's moderately well studied. It's dramatic when you look at it, and it has had an effect.

My daughter teaches in a state college where the students are mostly working class. They don't call themselves working class. She's not allowed to use the term—they're called middle class. Basically, they want to be nurses, police officers or skilled workers. She said she teaches labor history, and she says they just hate unions because they regard the union as something which forces you to go on strike, which steals your dues and doesn't do anything for you. As far as that's the case, they just hate unions.

Over the past few months, there has been a noticeable focus from activists on debt and its relationship to people's labor and livelihoods. While debt is not a new phenomenon, the level of analysis has become more detailed after the 2008 crash and the rise of the Occupy movement. There's the Jubilee Debt Campaign, which has campaigned for some time against sovereign debt clawed from impoverished countries. Strike Debt is developing ideas around the debtor as a new political subject. The Rolling Jubilee collectively purchased distressed medical debt on secondary markets in order to instantly write it off as an act of solidarity. These initiatives, along with the European We Won't Pay campaign, are some of the more recent movements against illegitimate debt that have grown to prominence.

Looking at the Rolling Jubilee, it also is a double-edged sword. On one hand, you are helping someone dramatically by abolishing their thousands of dollars worth of medical debt. So instead of debt collectors buying it on the market and saying, "You owe this amount of money" and giving you a principal balance and some other fee, you don't have to pay it back. But, on the other hand, you're giving $500,000 to speculators on the market.

And you're also undercutting the government responsibility to do it in the first place—political pressure that would lead them to do it. The same issue arises all the time. Let's say, with charity: When you give aid to homeless people, you're taking away the community responsibility to do it; and in a democratic society, that usually means the government. And this is true—you can't escape the world you're in; you can only try to change it. It's not an argument against giving to charities.

Absolutely. I don't want to use the term "morality," but there's definitely a sense that it's time to take action.

We are responsible to other people. We should at the same time—and I think that's what Occupy ought to be doing—create an understanding that there is a community responsibility. It's not our responsibility—we're doing it because the community isn't. It's like schools: There's community responsibility to make sure that kids go to school. People who want to privatize schools would be delighted if an individual charity sent particular kids to school. Then it wouldn't have to be a community responsibility, and it would cost them less in tax money. But I think much deeper than that is that they want to undermine the conception of communal responsibility. That also goes back 150 years, back to the beginning of the industrial revolution. It's remarkable to see how persistent it is, this idea that workers and working people were being driven from the farms into the factories.

In England, the same thing happened a century earlier, and they bitterly resented it. The labor press from that time is very striking. People should read it and reprint it. I mean, it's very radical. They had never heard of Marx, never heard of communists, but the press was just instinctively very radical.

They were opposed to wage labor and regarded it as not very different from slavery. The main thing they opposed was what they called the New Spirit of the Age: *You gain wealth, forgetting anybody else.* So that's what they've been driving into people's heads for 150 years. I talk to MIT students. Many are upwardly mobile students. A lot of them are kind of behind Ayn Rand: "Why should I do anything for anyone else? I should be after it for myself."

That sentiment has spread. Actually, I think that's what happened in Michigan. The anti-union feeling that has been built up is, "Why should that guy over there have a pension when I don't?" In Wisconsin, that feeling was very strong. The labor movement was never able to get across the fact that these guys are hard-working people who gave up their wages so they could have some benefits. They're not stealing from you. That never got across. So the very widespread feeling, even among union members, was, "They got a pension; they got tenure. I don't have a pension. I don't got tenure. I'm just out for myself. I don't care." And that's one of the problems with volunteer and popular activism: It builds a sense of solidarity among participants, but it undermines another sense of solidarity in the community at large. That's really significant. I think that's what underlies the massive attack against Social Security, which is really a bipartisan attack. Obama says we have to cut it, too. There's no economic problem, but Social Security is based on the conception that you care about other people. That argument has become unpopular. But you've got to drive that out of people's heads. You have to make sure not to contribute to that.

We were trying to think that, if we had to describe Occupy Wall Street and the protests of the last year in a very succinct kind of way, it would probably be based on the idea that, for generations prior, there was a sense of working-class solidarity and the idea of having collective power.

You're right, I thought the most important contribution of the Occupy movement was to re-create this mutual support system that was lacking in society. But it has this dual character: You have to figure out ways to do it that don't undermine the broader conception of solidarity. "Actual solidarity" is the slogan of the labor movement—well, it used to be.

With that in mind, if Strike Debt is taking this approach where it's focusing on debt, the commonality is that we're not all workers, but we're all debtors. Would you say that this is a rallying point?

Sure. There are many points of commonality among people—say, schools. I don't have kids who go to school. I suppose you don't either. But nevertheless, many of us, we're committed to making sure kids go to school. We're part of that community and lots of other communities.

But it's much easier to say, "You're a worker, you sell your labor for a wage." It's much easier to say that than it is to say, "You owe a debt and you have a solidarity to this person who also has debt." How do you articulate that bond of solidarity?

That's the obvious point of contact. That's the way health organizing ought to work: Everybody is going to face health problems.

It's obvious that there is a need for that kind of thinking. But I'm not sure that it's so obvious that you could communicate it to people and get people out on the street and organizing amongst themselves.

Well, you know, it certainly happened in other places. Again, Canada is not that different, but at least it had something of that concept of solidarity. That's how they got a national health system. That should have been a major educational issue, just like with pensions for public workers. They should have said, "Pension cuts mean that they cut back your wages." Almost nobody pointed it out. We're just losing a lot of opportunities.

The same thing has to be done about debt, as I'm sure you're doing it. A lot of the debt is just totally illegitimate. Take student debt. There's no economic basis for it. It is just a tactic of control. You can prove that there's no economic basis. Other countries don't have it. Poor countries don't have it. Rich countries don't have it. It exists only in the United States, so it can't be economically necessary. The United States was a much poorer country in the 1950s, much poorer, but it had basically free education.

Sure, the National Health System in the UK was founded after World War II when the debt was far greater in proportion to the nation's wealth.

Even in the United States, which came out of the war very rich, it was nowhere near as rich as it is today. But the GI Bill gave us free education. Yes, it was selective: only whites, very few women. But it was free education for a huge amount of people who would have never gone to school without it. In the 1940s, when I went to college, I went to an Ivy League school where the tuition cost was $100. That's a poor country, compared to today's standards.

THERE'S ALWAYS A CLASS WAR GOING ON

Chris Steele interview with Noam Chomsky

March 28, 2013, Cambridge, Massachusetts

An article that recently came out in Rolling Stone, *titled "Gangster Bankers: Too Big to Jail," by Matt Taibbi, asserts that the government is afraid to prosecute powerful bankers, such as those running HSBC. Taibbi says that there's "an arrestable class and an unarrestable class."* * *What is your view on the current state of class war in the U.S.?*

Well, there's always a class war going on. The

---

* "Americans have long understood that the rich get good lawyers and get off, while the poor suck eggs and do time. But this is something different. This is the government admitting to being afraid to prosecute the very powerful—something it never did even in the heydays of Al Capone or Pablo Escobar, something it didn't do even with Richard Nixon. And when you admit that some people are too important to prosecute, it's just a few short steps to the obvious corollary—that everybody else is unimportant enough to jail. An arrestable class and an unarrestable class. We always suspected it, now it's admitted. So what do we do?" Matt Taibbi, "Gangster Bankers: Too Big to Jail," *Rolling Stone*, February 14, 2013; www.rollingstone.com/politics/news/gangster-bankers-too-big-to-jail-20130214

United States, to an unusual extent, is a business-run society, more so than others. The business classes are very class-conscious—they're constantly fighting a bitter class war to improve their power and diminish opposition. Occasionally this is recognized.

We don't use the term "working class" here because it's a taboo term. You're supposed to say "middle class," because it helps diminish the understanding that there's a class war going on.

It's true that there was a one-sided class war, and that's because the other side hadn't chosen to participate, so the union leadership had for years pursued a policy of making a compact with the corporations, in which their workers, say the autoworkers—would get certain benefits like fairly decent wages, health benefits and so on. But it wouldn't engage the general class structure. In fact, that's one of the reasons why Canada has a national health program and the United States doesn't. The same unions on the other side of the border were calling for health care for everybody. Here they were calling for health care for themselves and they got it. Of course, it's a compact with corporations that the corporations can break anytime they want, and by the 1970s they were planning to break it and we've seen what has happened since.

This is just one part of a long and continuing

class war against working people and the poor. It's a war that is conducted by a highly class-conscious business leadership, and it's one of the reasons for the unusual history of the U.S. labor movement. In the U.S., organized labor has been repeatedly and extensively crushed, and has endured a very violent history as compared with other countries.

In the late 19th century there was a major union organization, Knights of Labor, and also a radical populist movement based on farmers. It's hard to believe, but it was based in Texas, and it was quite radical. They wanted their own banks, their own cooperatives, their own control over sales and commerce. It became a huge movement that spread over major farming areas.

The Farmers' Alliance did try to link up with the Knights of Labor, which would have been a major class-based organization if it had succeeded. But the Knights of Labor were crushed by violence, and the Farmers' Alliance was dismantled in other ways. As a result, one of the major popular democratic forces in American history was essentially dismantled. There are a lot of reasons for it, one of which was that the Civil War has never really ended. One effect of the Civil War was that the political parties that came out of it were sectarian parties, so the slogan was, "You vote where you shoot," and that remains the case.

Take a look at the red states and the blue states in the last election: It's the Civil War. They've changed party labels, but other than that, it's the same: sectarian parties that are not class-based because divisions are along different lines. There are a lot of reasons for it.

The enormous benefits given to the very wealthy, the privileges for the very wealthy here, are way beyond those of other comparable societies and are part of the ongoing class war. Take a look at CEO salaries. CEOs are no more productive or brilliant here than they are in Europe, but the pay, bonuses, and enormous power they get here are out of sight. They're probably a drain on the economy, and they become even more powerful when they are able to gain control of policy decisions.

That's why we have a sequester over the deficit and not over jobs, which is what really matters to the population. But it doesn't matter to the banks, so the heck with it. It also illustrates the considerable shredding of the whole system of democracy. So, by now, they rank people by income level or wages roughly the same: The bottom 70 percent or so are virtually disenfranchised; they have almost no influence on policy, and as you move up the scale you get more influence. At the very top, you basically run the show.

A good topic to research, if possible, would be

"why people don't vote." Nonvoting is very high, roughly 50 percent, even in presidential elections—much higher in others. The attitudes of people who don't vote are studied. First of all, they mostly identify themselves as Democrats. And if you look at their attitudes, they are mostly Social Democratic. They want jobs, they want benefits, they want the government to be involved in social services and so on, but they don't vote, partly, I suppose, because of the impediments to voting. It's not a big secret. Republicans try really hard to prevent people from voting, because the more that people vote, the more trouble they are in. There are other reasons why people don't vote. I suspect, but don't know how to prove, that part of the reason people don't vote is they just know their votes don't make any difference, so why make the effort? So you end up with a kind of plutocracy in which the public opinion doesn't matter much. It is not unlike other countries in this respect, but more extreme. All along, it's more extreme. So yes, there is a constant class war going on.

The case of labor is crucial, because it is the base of organization of any popular opposition to the rule of capital, and so it has to be dismantled. There's a tax on labor all the time. During the 1920s, the labor movement was virtually smashed by Wilson's Red Scare and other things. In the 1930s, it reconstituted and was the driving force of the New Deal, with the CIO organizing and so on. By the late 1930s, the business classes were organizing to try to react to this. They began, but couldn't do much during the war, because things were on hold, but immediately after the war it picked up with the Taft-Hartley Act and huge propaganda campaigns, which had massive effect. Over the years, the effort to undermine the unions and labor generally succeeded. By now, private-sector unionization is very low, partly because, since Reagan, government has pretty much told employers, "You know you can violate the laws, and we're not going to do anything about it." Under Clinton, NAFTA offered a method for employers to illegally undermine labor organizing by threatening to move enterprises to Mexico. A number of illegal operations by employers shot up at that time. What's left are private-sector unions, and they're under bipartisan attack.

They've been protected somewhat because the federal laws did function for the public-sector unions, but now they're under bipartisan attack. When Obama declares a pay freeze for federal workers, that's actually a tax on federal workers. It comes to the same thing, and, of course, this is right at the time we say that we can't raise taxes on the very rich. Take the last tax agreement where the Republicans claimed, "We already gave up tax increases." Take a look at what happened. Raising the payroll tax, which is a tax on working people, is much more of a tax increase than raising taxes on the super-rich, but that passed quietly because we don't look at those things.

The same is happening across the board. There are major efforts being made to dismantle Social Security, the public schools, the post office—anything that benefits the population has to be dismantled. Efforts against the U.S. Postal Service are particularly surreal. I'm old enough to remember the Great Depression, a time when the country was quite poor but there were still postal deliveries. Today, post offices, Social Security, and public schools all have to be dismantled because they are seen as being based on a principle that is regarded as extremely dangerous.

If you care about other people, that's now a very dangerous idea. If you care about other people, you might try to organize to undermine power and authority. That's not going to happen if you care only about yourself. Maybe you can become rich, but you don't care whether other people's kids can go to school, or can afford food to eat, or things like that. In the United States, that's called "libertarian" for some wild reason. I mean, it's actually highly authoritarian, but that doctrine is extremely important for power systems as a way of atomizing and undermining the public.

That's why unions had the slogan, "solidarity," even though they may not have lived up to it. And that's what really counts: solidarity, mutual aid, care for one another and so on. And it's really important for power systems to undermine that ideologically, so huge efforts go into it. Even trying to stimulate consumerism is an effort to undermine it. Having a market society automatically carries with it an undermining of solidarity. For example, in the market system you have a choice: You can buy a Toyota or you can buy a Ford, but you can't buy a subway because that's not offered. Market systems don't offer common goods; they offer private consumption. If you want a subway, you're going to have to get together with other people and make a collective decision. Otherwise, it's simply not an option within the market system, and as democracy is increasingly undermined, it's less and less of an option within the public system. All of these things converge, and they're all part of general class war.

Can you give some insight on how the labor movement could rebuild in the United States?

Well, it's been done before. Each time labor has been attacked—and as I said, in the 1920s the labor movement was practically destroyed—popular efforts were able to reconstitute it. That can happen again. It's not going to be easy. There are institutional barriers, ideological barriers, cultural barriers. One big problem is that the white working class has been pretty much abandoned by the political system. The Democrats don't even try to organize them anymore. The Republicans claim to do it; they get most of the vote, but they do it on non-economic issues, on non-labor issues. They often try to mobilize them on the grounds of issues steeped in racism and sexism and so on, and here the liberal policies of the 1960s had a harmful effect because of some of the ways in which they were carried out. There are some pretty good studies of this. Take busing to integrate schools. In principle, it made some sense, if you wanted to try to overcome segregated schools. Obviously, it didn't work. Schools are probably more segregated now for all kinds of reasons, but the way it was originally done undermined class solidarity.

For example, in Boston there was a program for integrating the schools through busing, but the way it worked was restricted to urban Boston, downtown Boston. So black kids were sent to the Irish neighborhoods and conversely, but the suburbs were left out. The suburbs are more affluent, professional and so on, so they were kind of out of it. Well, what happens when you send black kids into an Irish neighborhood? What happens when some Irish telephone linemen who have worked all their lives finally got enough money to buy small houses in a neighborhood where they want to send their kids to the local school and cheer for the local football team and have a community, and so on? All of a sudden, some of their kids are being sent out, and black kids are coming in. How do you think at least some of these guys will feel? At least some end up being racists. The suburbs are out of it, so they can cluck their tongues about how racist everyone is elsewhere, and that kind of pattern was carried out all over the country.

The same has been true of women's rights. But when you have a working class that's under real pressure, you know, people are going to say that rights are being undermined, that jobs are being undermined. Maybe the one thing that the white working man can hang onto is that he runs his home? Now that that's being taken away and nothing is being offered, he's not part of the program of advancing women's rights. That's fine for college professors, but it has a different effect in working-class areas. It doesn't have to be that way. It depends on how it's done, and it was done in a way that simply undermined natural solidarity. There are a lot of factors that play into it, but by this point it's going to be pretty hard to organize the working class on the grounds that should really concern them: common solidarity, common welfare.

In some ways, it shouldn't be too hard, because these attitudes are really prized by most of the population. If you look at Tea Party members, the kind that say, "Get the government off my back, I want a small government" and so on, when their attitudes are studied, it turns out that they're mostly social democratic. You know, people are human after all. So yes, you want more money for health, for help, for people who need it and so on and so forth, but "I don't want the government, get that off my back" and related attitudes are tricky to overcome.

Some polls are pretty amazing. There was one conducted in the South right before the presidential elections. Just Southern whites, I think, were asked about the economic plans of the two candidates, Barack Obama and Mitt Romney. Southern whites said they preferred Romney's plan, but when asked about its particular components, they opposed every one. Well, that's the effect of good propaganda: getting people not to think in terms of their own interests, let alone the interest of communities and the class they're part of. Overcoming that takes a lot of work. I don't think it's impossible, but it's not going to happen easily.

In a recent article about the Magna Carta and the

Charter of the Forest,* you discuss Henry Vane, who was beheaded for drafting a petition that called the people's power "the original from whence all just power arises." Would you agree the coordinated repression of Occupy was like the beheading of Vane?

Occupy hasn't been treated nicely, but we shouldn't exaggerate. Compared with the kind of repression that usually goes on, it wasn't that severe. Just ask people who were part of the civil rights movement in the early 1960s, in the South, let's say. It was incomparably worse, as was just showing up at anti-war demonstrations where people were getting maced and beaten and so on. Activist groups get repressed. Power systems don't pat them on the head. Occupy was treated badly, but not off the spectrum—in fact, in some ways not as bad as others. I wouldn't draw exaggerated comparisons. It's not like beheading somebody who says, "Let's have popular power."

How does the Charter of the Forest relate to environmental and indigenous resistance to the Keystone XL pipeline?

A lot. The Charter of the Forest, which was half

---

* Noam Chomsky, "Destroying the Commons: How the Magna Carta Became a Minor Carta," *TomDispatch.com*, July 22, 2012. www.tomdispatch.com/blog/175571/

the Magna Carta, has more or less been forgotten. The forest didn't just mean the woods. It meant common property, the source of food, fuel. It was a common possession, so it was cared for. The forests were cultivated in common and kept functioning, because they were part of people's common possessions, their source of livelihood, and even a source of dignity. That slowly collapsed in England under the enclosure movements, the state efforts to shift to private ownership and control. In the United States it happened differently, but the privatization is similar. What you end up with is the widely held belief, now standard doctrine, that's called "the tragedy of the commons" in Garrett Hardin's phrase. According to this view, if things are held in common and aren't privately owned, they're going to be destroyed. History shows the exact opposite: When things were held in common, they were preserved and maintained. But, according to the capitalist ethic, if things aren't privately owned, they're going to be ruined, and that's "the tragedy of the commons." So, therefore, you have to put everything under private control and take it away from the public, because the public is just going to destroy it.

Now, how does that relate to the environmental problem? Very significantly: the commons are the environment. When they're a common possession—not owned, but everybody holds them together in a community—they're preserved, sustained and cultivated for the next generation. If they're privately owned, they're going to be destroyed for profit; that's what private ownership is, and that's exactly what's happening today.

What you say about the indigenous population is very striking. There's a major problem that the whole species is facing. A likelihood of serious disaster may be not far off. We are approaching a kind of tipping point, where climate change becomes irreversible. It could be a couple of decades, maybe less, but the predictions are constantly being shown to be too conservative. It is a very serious danger; no sane person can doubt it. The whole species is facing a real threat for the first time in its history of serious disaster, and there are some people trying to do something about it and there are others trying to make it worse. Who are they? Well, the ones who are trying to make it better are the pre-industrial societies, the pre-technological societies, the indigenous societies, the First Nations. All around the world, these are the communities that are trying to preserve the rights of nature.

The rich societies, like the United States and Canada, are acting in ways to bring about disaster as quickly as possible. That's what it means, for example, when both political parties and the press talk enthusiastically about "a century of energy independence." "Energy independence" doesn't mean a damn thing, but put that aside. A century of "energy independence" means that we make sure that every bit of Earth's fossil fuels comes out of the ground and we burn it. In societies that have large indigenous populations, like, for example, Ecuador, an oil producer, people are trying to get support for keeping the oil in the ground. They want funding so as to keep the oil where it ought to be. We, however, have to get everything out of the ground, including tar sands, then burn it, which makes things as bad as possible as quickly as possible. So you have this odd situation where the educated, "advanced" civilized people are trying to cut everyone's throats as quickly as possible and the indigenous, less educated, poorer populations are trying to prevent the disaster. If somebody was watching this from Mars, they'd think this species was insane.

As far as a free, democracy-centered society, self-organization seems possible on small scales. Do you think it is possible on a larger scale and with human rights and quality of life as a standard, and if so, what community have you visited that seems closest to an example to what is possible?

Well, there are a lot of things that are possible. I have visited some examples that are pretty large scale, in fact, very large scale. Take Spain, which is in a huge economic crisis. But one part of Spain is doing okay—that's the Mondragón collective. It's a big conglomerate involving banks, industry, housing, all sorts of things. It's worker owned, not worker managed, so partial industrial democracy, but it exists in a capitalist economy, so it's doing all kinds of ugly things like exploiting foreign labor and so on. But economically and socially, it's flourishing as compared with the rest of the society and other societies. It is very large, and that can be done anywhere. It certainly can be done here. In fact, there are tentative explorations of contacts between the Mondragón and the United Steelworkers, one of the more progressive unions, to think about developing comparable structures here, and it's being done to an extent.

The one person who has written very well about this is Gar Alperovitz, who is involved in organizing work around enterprises in parts of the old Rust Belt, which are pretty successful and could be spread just as a cooperative could be spread. There are really no limits to it other than willingness to participate, and that is, as always, the problem. If you're willing to adhere to the task and gauge yourself, there's no limit.

Actually, there's a famous sort of paradox posed by David Hume centuries ago. Hume is one of the founders of classical liberalism. He's an important philosopher and a political philosopher. He said that if you take a look at societies around the world—any of them—power is in the hands of the governed, those who are being ruled. Hume asked, why don't they use that power and overthrow the masters and take control? He says, the answer has to be that, in all societies, the most brutal, the most free, the governed can be controlled by control of opinion. If you can control their attitudes and beliefs and separate them from one another and so on, then they won't rise up and overthrow you.

That does require a qualification. In the more brutal and repressive societies, controlling opinion is less important, because you can beat people with a stick. But as societies become more free, it becomes more of a problem, and we see that historically. The societies that develop the most expansive propaganda systems are also the most free societies.

The most extensive propaganda system in the world is the public relations industry, which developed in Britain and the United States. A century ago, dominant sectors recognized that enough freedom had been won by the population. They reasoned that it's hard to control people by force, so they had to do it by turning the attitudes and opinions of the population with propaganda and other devices of separation and marginalization, and so on. Western powers have become highly skilled in this.

In the United States, the advertising and public relations industry is huge. Back in the more honest days, they called it propaganda. Now the term doesn't sound nice, so it's not used anymore, but it's basically a huge propaganda system which is designed very extensively for quite specific purposes.

First of all, it has to undermine markets by trying to create irrational, uninformed consumers who will make irrational choices. That's what advertising is about, the opposite of what a market is supposed to be, and anybody who turns on a television set can see that for themselves. It has to do with monopolization and product differentiation, all sorts of things, but the point is that you have to drive the population to irrational consumption, which does separate them from one another.

As I said, consumption is individual, so it's not done as an act of solidarity—so you don't have ads on television saying, "Let's get together and build a mass transportation system." Who's going to fund that? The other thing they need to do is undermine democracy the same way, so they run campaigns, political campaigns mostly run by PR agents. It's very clear what they have to do. They have to create uninformed voters who will make irrational decisions, and that's what the campaigns are about. Billions of dollars go into it, and the idea is to shred democracy, restrict markets to service the rich, and make sure the power gets concentrated, that capital gets concentrated and the people are driven to irrational and self-destructive behavior. And it is self-destructive, often dramatically so. For example, one of the first achievements of the U.S. public relations system back in the 1920s was led, incidentally, by a figure honored by Wilson, Roosevelt and Kennedy—liberal progressive Edward Bernays.

His first great success was to induce women to smoke. In the 1920s, women didn't smoke. So here's this big population which was not buying cigarettes, so he paid young models to march down New York City's Fifth Avenue holding cigarettes. His message to women was, "You want to be cool like a model? You should smoke a cigarette." How many millions of corpses did that create? I'd hate to calculate it. But it was considered an enormous success. The same is true of the murderous character of corporate propaganda with tobacco, asbestos, lead, chemicals, vinyl chloride, across the board. It is just shocking, but PR is a very honored profession, and it does control people and undermine their options of working together. And so that's Hume's paradox, but people don't have to submit to it. You can see through it and struggle against it.

THE MORE SOLIDARITY SPREADS, THE MORE YOU CAN DO

Free Speech Radio News interview with Noam Chomsky

May 2, 2013, Cambridge, Massachusetts

The mainstream media rarely mention people-driven solutions to the world's problems, so we'd like to talk to you about just that today. Let's start with the labor movement. You've talked about the effectiveness of sit-down strikes in which workers occupy a workplace as a precursor to taking it over. You've said, with enough popular support, sit-down strikes can work and be the basis for a real revolution. But how much popular support is needed and what should it look like?

Well, it has to be extensive. Actually, it can work. I happen to have just come back from Ireland, and one of the things I did there was meet with a group of workers at a plant called Vita Cortex. I'd been supporting their strike. They had a long sit-down strike. The management wanted to sell the plant, a profitable plant, to some rich entrepreneur who would move it somewhere else. All the workers were just going to be fired. Some of them had long tenure. They got together, formed a community support group and sat in on the plant. And there was community support—people wanted to keep them there. People brought food and all kinds of help. And they won, after, I think, about six months. The owner agreed to keep it there, pay the workers and so on.

And that was in Ireland?

That was in Cork, southern Ireland. And it was doing okay, not hugely profitable. Ireland is in a big downturn, so this was serious. But they won. They didn't get everything, but a lot. It can be done. Much of the New Deal legislation, which was important, was motivated by employee concerns, and other concerns, when CIO organizing, which was new then, reached the point where it was leading to sit-down strikes—because sit-down strikes drive fear into management and everyone else. If we're sitting in and doing nothing, why shouldn't we run the factory? We're the ones who know how to run the place, so let's run it and kick out the bosses. That's only one step away.

Why are they so rare in the United States?

Strikes of any kind are very rare, especially since Reagan, who kind of broke the mandate against using scabs. That's outlawed everywhere in the world. I think maybe apartheid South Africa allowed it. But when Reagan broke the flight-controllers' strike, he set the tone, and maybe ten years later there was a strike at a major Caterpillar manufacturing plant. I think it was in Peoria, and management broke it by bringing in scabs. Now that's illegal everywhere in the world. As I said, apartheid South Africa I think allowed it, but it passed.

It's kind of interesting what happened. The *Chicago Tribune*, which is a conservative news-paper but covered labor affairs pretty well, had a lot of coverage about Peoria and the scandal of bringing in scabs. Well, that was maybe twenty years ago. When President Obama—who was in Chicago at the time, so he couldn't have missed it—decided to show his solidarity with workers, he went to that plant and nobody commented on it. It's effaced from memory. And the labor movement, as you know, has been decimated. It developed enormously in the 1930s and it's responsible for most of the progressive legislation that took place. There was an immediate backlash, even by the late 1930s. That's when management initiated what are now called sci-entific methods of strike breaking, sophisticated strike-breaking techniques.

What are some of those?

Some of them are called the Mohawk Valley formula. Say there is some town in Pennsylvania where there's a strike going on. The idea is to saturate the town with propaganda whose basic theme is Americanism: We're all Americans, we all work together, we all love each other. We're all helping the friendly boss who works to the bone eighty hours a day for the service of the workers, the banker who loves to give you money to buy a car, and the workman with his pail going to work and his wife who's making dinner at home. They're all one big happy family living in harmony. And then these outsiders come in, the union organizers, and there's a hint as well that they're probably communists, and they're trying to disrupt the harmony and prevent everyone from living the good American dream. That's basically the theme, and the idea is to saturate everything with propaganda: the schools, the churches, everything. And it sometimes has an effect. That's one technique. There are others.

These developed substantially under Reagan, who was very anti-labor. In fact, he hated poor people with a passion. So, for example, during the lettuce strike, Reagan was governor of California. He very ostentatiously appeared on television happily eating lettuce just to show what he thought about the striking workers, the poorest of the poor. If he can kick them in the face, great. He loved that. Just like his "welfare queen" business, which demonized welfare and portrayed rich black women being driven in their Cadillacs to the welfare offices and stealing your money, and that sort of thing. In fact, he made it very clear. You couldn't miss it.

Reagan opened his campaign in Philadelphia, Mississippi, a little town which is probably unknown except for one thing: There was a massacre of civil rights workers there. And that's where he very ostentatiously opened his campaign—telling people: Don't worry, I'm a racist thug. And then came the strike. But his administration also informed the business world that the government essentially wasn't going to apply the laws. There are laws about illegal interference with union organizing and they're obviously supposed to implement them. But he made it quite clear that you can do what you like. Illegal measures, like firing of union organizers, went way up during the Reagan years. I think it might have tripled, and it continued.

Then came Clinton, who had a different technique for undermining unions. It was called NAFTA. There have been studies on the effect of NAFTA on strike breaking in the United States, and it's substantial. It's illegal, but if you have a criminal state, you can do what you like—you don't enforce the laws. So a standard technique would be, say, if there's an organizing campaign somewhere, for management to tell workers, "You guys can go and strike if you want, but if you win, it's all going to Mexico." That's a very effective technique. In the absence of solidarity, real solidarity, in fact international solidarity, it's a pretty effective technique of strike breaking, and the number of illegal strike-breaking efforts, I think, went up by about 50 percent after NAFTA.

All this started right after the Second World War with Taft-Hartley, the huge anti-labor campaigns and so on. Now there are companies which just do strike breaking. There are scientific and sophisticated techniques, and there's plenty of clout behind it, a huge amount of corporate money, and the government supports it. And there isn't much popular support. You could see it in the passage of the right-to-work law in Michigan, which was pretty shocking. That's a labor state, and it turned that out a lot of union members voted for it. If you look at the propaganda, you can see why. First of the all, the very phrase "right to work": It's actually not right to work; it's right to scrounge. What it means is a person can work in a factory and refuse to join the union so he doesn't have to pay dues, and he'll get all the protection that the union offers to others, the grievances and so on. He gets the protection, but doesn't pay. That's all that right-to-work means.

It's a technique for destroying labor. But the propaganda has been effective, and it's best against public workers, librarians, firefighters, teachers or even workers in a unionized plant. They have jobs, they get pensions, they get health care. You are unemployed, you can't a job. And if you get one, it's part-time and you don't get a pension. So they're stealing from you, especially the public service workers who are leaning on taxes. They're underpaid, relative to their skill level, and the reason they get pensions is because they take lower pay. It's a trade-off. They say, okay, we'll take lower wages, but you guarantee us our pension. But the propaganda works, and the administrations supported it.

When Obama declares a freeze on pay for federal workers, he's saying that we're not going to raise taxes on the rich but that we are going to raise taxes on you, because a freeze on public workers is identical to a tax increase. The whole technique of demonizing labor and "corrupt union leaders"—I mean, this goes way back.

In the early 1950s there were two movies that came out about the same time. One was *Salt of the Earth*, a marvelous low-budget movie. It was about a strike that was eventually won. I think a Mexican woman was leading it. It was a very well-done movie, but nobody ever heard of it. There was another movie that came out at the same time called *On the Waterfront*, starring Marlon Brando, and it was about a corrupt union leader and the good, honest workman, you know, Joe with his pail and stuff. They finally got together. Marlon Brando kind of organized them, and the thing ends up with Marlon Brando throwing the union organizer into the ocean or something like that. Now that was a big hit. Incidentally, it was directed by Elia Kazan, who was supposedly a rather progressive director. But the point was to get people to hate the unions because they're all a bunch of corrupt gangsters and they're just stealing from you honest workmen and so on. And this is just one piece of an enormous campaign. By the time some of the scholarship came out on it, I was shocked by the scale. I had been following it, but had no idea. And it's had an effect.

One solution, since labor has been weakened, is for workers to start their own worker-run and worker-managed businesses. A lot of people were inspired by the growth of worker-run collectives and businesses in Argentina following the 2001 economic collapse there. In the United States, there are about several hundred, including Free Speech Radio News, which has been worker-run and worker-managed since it was founded thirteen years ago. Do you think this could grow and expand in the United States?

It's quite significant. There's been very good work on this, which ought to be read, by Gar Alperovitz, who is both an activist and a writer, a very good historian. What I know of, it's mostly around northern Ohio and the Rust Belt, and what happened there is interesting and worth thinking about. The steelworkers union, which is one of the more progressive in some ways—not without plenty of problems—are working on some sort of an arrangement with Mondragón, which is this huge, worker-owned conglomerate in the Basque country in northern Spain.

And that's been around since the 1950s, right?

Goes back to the 1950s as church-initiated, what became liberation theology and so on. But there's also a strong workers' tradition there, going way back to the Spanish Revolution. And it's grown and developed. It's now a number of productive enterprises: banks, housing, schools, hospitals. It's quite an elaborate affair. And it seems to be withstanding the financial crisis, while everything else in Spain is collapsing. I don't know the details, but that's what it looks like. It's not worker-managed. Workers select management, who then act on their own. And, of course, it's part of an international capitalist economy which means that you can argue the ethics of it, since they do things like exploit labor abroad and so on. They say that they have to do it to compete and survive—maybe—that you can't extricate yourself from the world you're in.

Of course, the more solidarity spreads, the more you can do things about that, but that's not easy. It's hard enough to reconstruct the labor movement internally. After all, every labor movement is called an international. That's an aspiration. It's a real problem in the United States. You could see it yesterday. Yesterday was May Day. I happened to get a letter in the morning. A ton of email comes in—one of them was from a friend in Brazil who told me that she wouldn't be going to work that day because it's a holiday, a labor holiday. In fact, it's a labor holiday all over the world, except in the United States where nobody knows what it is. I happened to be giving a talk at Harvard in the afternoon and this came up. I asked the big audience of Harvard graduate students, "What do you think May Day is?" And some people said, "You mean dance around the May pole," or something like that. It's not only a labor holiday. It's a labor holiday that was initiated in support of American workers who were struggling for an eight-hour day and who were among the most oppressed in the industrial world.

So here's this holiday—you know, big demonstrations everywhere, and all kinds of celebrations and so on, and here nobody knows what it is. That's a sign of extremely effective indoctrination. It's the kind of thing that we just have to work our way out of. Here there are some small celebrations. Maybe Occupy might have had a May Day march or something. And it's kind of interesting the way the press treated it. Usually they just ignore it. But if you take a look at the *New York Times* the next day, it had an article that said demonstrations were in support of labor or something. But it was datelined "Havana," and there was a picture of a huge mob of Cubans marching and some commentary. It was clear what the implication is: This holiday is some kind of commie business; it's got nothing to do with us. I don't know if it's conscious or if it's just so internalized that the journalists don't even see what they're doing. But the message was, "Forget it, it's some alien thing."

It's like breaking up the harmony in your town when the union organizers come in; it's kind of that imagery. And here, strikingly, we do have a Labor Day, but notice what day it is. It's the day when you go back to work, not the day when you struggle for your rights. The success of indoctrination in the United States is really amazing.

I wanted to talk about that a little bit. It's been twenty-five years since the publication of your and Edward Herman's acclaimed book Manufacturing Consent. *How much do you think has changed with the propaganda model, and where do you see it playing out most prominently today?*

Well, ten years ago we had a re-edition and we talked about some of the changes. One change is that we were too narrow. There are a number of filters that determine the framework of reporting, and one of the filters was too narrow. Instead of "anti-communism," which was too narrow, it should have been "fear of the concocted enemy." So yes, it could be anti-communism—most of that is concocted. So take Cuba again. It's hard to believe, but for the Pentagon, Cuba was listed as one of the military threats to the United States until a couple of years ago. This is so ludicrous; you don't even know whether to laugh or cry. It's as if the Soviet Union had listed Luxembourg as a threat to its security. But here it kind of passes.

The United States is a very frightened country. And there are all kinds of things concocted for you to be frightened about. So that should have been the filter, and [there were] a few other things, but I think it's basically the same.

There is change. Free Speech Radio didn't exist when we wrote the book, and there are some things on the Internet which break the bonds, as do independent work and things like the book I was just talking about when we came in, Jeremy Scahill's *Dirty Wars*, which is a fantastic piece of investigative reporting on the ground of what actually happens in the countries where we're carrying out these terror campaigns. And there's a lot of talk about drones, but not much about the fact that they are terror weapons.

If we were sitting here wondering if, all of a sudden, there's going to be a bomb in this room, because they maybe want to kill him or kill us or whatever, it's terrorizing. In fact, we just saw a dramatic example of this which got a couple lines in the paper. A few days after the Boston Marathon bombing, there was a drone attack on a village in Yemen, kind of an isolated village. Obama and his friends decided to murder some guy. So the villagers are sitting there, and suddenly this guy gets blown away and whoever else is around him. I don't think it was reported except for the fact that there was Senate testimony a week later by a person from the village who's quite respected by Jeremy and others who know him. The man, Farea al-Muslimi, who studied at a high school in the U.S., testified to the Senate and he described what happened to his village. He said that everybody knew the man that they murdered, and that they could have easily apprehended him, but it was easier to kill him and terrify the village. He also said something else which is important. He said that his friends and neighbors used to know of the United States primarily through his stories of "the wonderful experiences" he had here.* He said the U.S. bombing has turned them into people who hate America and want revenge—that's all it takes. And, in fact, this whole terror system is creating enemies and threats faster than it's killing suspects, apart from how awful that is. These things are going on, and going back to Jeremy, his book exposes a lot of it and also the exploits of the secret executive army, JSOC, Joint Special Operations Command. It's dangerous, but it's the kind of thing an investigative reporter could do, and he's done it. There's more of it now, fortunately, in some respects, than there was then.

So, some progress.

Yes. On the other hand, the indoctrination system has gotten incredibly powerful. The examples that I mentioned, like the right-to-work laws—it is pretty shocking that that can succeed. So, I'd say it's about the same.

---

* Charlie Savage, "Drone Strikes Turn Allies Into Enemies, Yemeni Says," *New York Times*, published April 23, 2013. www.nytimes.com/2013/04/24/world/middleeast/judiciary-panel-hears-testimony-on-use-of-drones.html?_r=0.

Income inequality entered the national dialogue with the Occupy movement, but the wealth gap for black and Latino families rarely generates debate or headlines. What role should the media—particularly independent media—play in ensuring critical public interest issues like these are at the forefront?

Independent media ought to be telling the truth about things that matter. That's quite different from the task of the commercial media. They have a task. They're supposed to be objective, and objectivity has a meaning in the world of journalism. In fact, it's taught in journalism schools. Objectivity means reporting honestly and accurately what's going on within the Beltway, inside the government. So that sets the bounds. There are Democrats and there are Republicans. Report honestly what they're saying—balance and so on—and then you're objective. If you go beyond that and you ask a question about the bounds, then you're biased, subjective, emotional, maybe anti-American, whatever the usual curse words are. So that's a task and, you know, you can understand it from the point of view of established power. It's a distorting prism with enormous impact. Even just the framework of what's looked at.

Take, for example, current domestic issues. We have "the sequester," which is harming the economy, and that's, in fact, conceded. But what's it about? Well, it's about the deficit. Who cares about the deficit? Banks, rich people and so on. What does the population care about? Jobs. In fact, this has even been studied. There are a couple of professional studies that tested this question. It turns out that concern about the deficit increases with wealth, and the reason is rich people are concerned that maybe someday in the future there might be a little bit of inflation, which is not good for lenders. It's fine for borrowers. So, therefore, we have to worry about the deficit, even if it destroys jobs.

The population has quite different views. They say, no, we want jobs. And they're right. Jobs mean stimulating demand, and government's got to do that. Corporations have money coming out of their ears, but they're not investing it because there's no demand. Consumers can't fill the gap because they're suffering from the impact of the crimes that the banks carried out. Of course, the corporations are richer than ever. That's the way it works, but it's not what's discussed within the Beltway. So you get some little comment on it around the fringes, but the focus has to be on the terrible problem of the deficit, which will maybe be a problem someday in the future, but not very serious.

In fact, professional political science has done

a pretty good job on a specific topic relative to this. This is a very heavily polled country, so you get to know a lot about public attitudes, and there are quite good studies on the relation between public attitudes and public policy and differentiating attitudes. And it turns out that maybe 70 percent of the population, the lower 70 percent on the wealth income level, are disenfranchised. That is, their opinions have no influence on policy. Senators don't pay any attention to them.

As you move up in income level you get more influence. When you get to the very top, and here the Occupy movement was a little misleading— it's not one percent, it's a tenth of a percent. When you get to the top tenth of a percent, where there's a huge concentration of wealth, you can't even talk about influence. They get what they want. That's why the banks who created the crisis, often with criminal action, are not only scot-free, but richer, more powerful and bigger than ever. Reading the business press, you can see there's a criminal action here and there, and maybe a slap on the wrist or something there.

Because of that, what's within the Beltway reflects wealth and power. Elections are basically bought. We know the story. So "objectivity" in the commercial media means looking at the world from the point of view of the extremely rich and powerful in the corporate sector. Now, it's not 100 percent from their view. There are a lot of very honest reporters who do all kinds of things. I read the national press and learn from them and so on, but it's very much skewed in that direction. It's kind of like the filters in *Manufacturing Consent*. And going back to your point, what the independent press ought to be doing is what the national press ought to be doing, looking at the world from the point of view of its population. This holds on issue after issue—you can almost pick it at random.

The Occupy movement has had several pretty big successes: Occupy Sandy, Occupy Our Homes, Strike Debt and the Rolling Jubilee. But what do you think a post-Occupy movement looks like? What comes next?

The Occupy tactic was a remarkably successful tactic. If I'd been asked a month before Zuccotti Park whether to do this, I would have said, you're crazy. But it worked extremely well. It just lighted a fire all over the place. People were just waiting for something to light the spark. And it was extremely successful, but it's a tactic, and tactics are not strategies. A tactic has a half-life; it has diminishing returns. And in particular, a tactic like this is going to arouse antagonism, because people don't want their lives disrupted and so on. It will be easy to fan it the way you do with public workers. So it's a tactic that had to be revised. Frankly, when the police broke the occupations up, it was harsh and brutal and didn't have to be done like that. But in some ways, it wasn't a bad thing, because it turned people to what they have to do next. And what they have to do next is bring it to the general population. Take up the topics that really bother people. Be there when you're needed like Sandy. Be there for the foreclosures. Focus on debt. Focus on a financial transaction tax, which ought to be instituted. Nobody else is bringing it up. That's what the Occupy movement ought to be doing, and not just as a national movement, but as an international movement.

It's actually striking that there are Occupy offshoots all over the world. I've talked at Occupy movements in Sydney, Australia, and England, all over. Everywhere you go there's something. And they link with other things that are happening, like the Indignados in Spain; the student actions in Chile, which are pretty remarkable; things in Greece, which are enormous; and even movements in the peripheral parts of Europe trying to struggle against the brutal austerity regimes, which are worse than here and which are just strangling the economies and destroying the European social contract. We look progressive in comparison with Europe.

So that's a future that can be looked forward

to, including things like we were talking about before, supporting and maybe even initiating things like worker-owned, worker-managed enterprises. It sounds reformist, but it's revolutionary. That's changing—at least giving the germs for changing—the basic structure of this society in a fundamental way. Why should banks own the enterprise in which people work? What business is it of theirs? Why should they decide whether you move it to Mexico or Bangladesh or where the next place will be? Why shouldn't the workers decide, or the communities? There's a lot to say about this.

Just consider, for example, the things that aren't being discussed in the immigration struggle. We're here in Boston, right? Right around Boston, there's a pretty large community of Mayan immigrants. They're still coming right now. They live right near here, but under the radar because they're undocumented. Why are Mayans coming here? They don't want to be here. Some of them I know pretty well, and when you talk to them, they say, "We'd rather be home." They don't want to be here.

Why are they coming? Well, because in the early 1980s, there was a virtually genocidal attack on the highlands in Guatemala that was supported by Ronald Reagan, backed by the United States. It practically wiped the place out, and there are now actually trials going on in Guatemala of the perpetrators, but nobody here talks about it. So, you know, we destroy their country and people flee because they can't survive. In fact, there's an interesting book coming out by David Bacon, who is an immigration activist. It's called *The Right to Stay Home.*

It was obvious, for example, that NAFTA was going to destroy Mexican agriculture. The Mexican campesinos can be as efficient as they like, but they can't compete with highly subsidized U.S agribusiness, and that means people are going to flee. And, in fact, it's not just coincidental that the year NAFTA was passed, Clinton started militarizing the border. It was an open border before, and so, of course, people are going to come. Well, these topics aren't discussed.

If you're worried about immigration, let's take a look at why people are coming and what our responsibility is and what we can do about it. They don't want to be here. And the same is true about exporting factories. People ought to have jobs in Bangladesh, but we ought to be paying attention to the fact that they have decent working conditions. They want it, we should want it, and we should struggle to make sure they have it. And then decisions can be made about a workforce and where they want their enterprise to be. There are all kinds of topics like this that free, independent media can bring up and movements like Occupy can be dedicated to.

MOVEMENT PROTEST SUPPORT
by NATIONAL LAWYERS GUILD

Thousands of people have been arrested exercising their freedom of speech and assembly while participating in Occupy actions. If you or someone you know needs legal assistance or has been the victim of excessive police force or brutality at a protest or gathering, contact the National Lawyers Guild, a non-profit federation of lawyers, legal workers and law students who join in at Occupy protests and monitor police activity on the street and in jail. The Guild has been providing invaluable legal advice to movement folks who get inadvertently arrested at protests, as well as those who consciously commit civil disobedience.

"What laws and police practices should I know about?"

You have First Amendment rights to protest lawfully. You have the right to hand out leaflets, rally on a sidewalk, and set up a moving picket line, so long as you do not block building entrances or more than half the sidewalk. The law requires a permit to march in the street, rally in a park with 20 or more people, or use electronic sound amplification. In New York, a "Mask Law" makes it unlawful for three or more people to wear masks, including bandanas: the NYPD aggressively enforces this law. Police will seize signs on wooden sticks, metal, and pvc piping—it's OK to attach signs to cardboard tubing. The police will not allow placing signs on fences or trees. If you hang a banner from a bridge over a highway, you risk arrest for Reckless Endangerment.

"What do I do if the police talk to me?"

You have a constitutional right to remain silent. If the police try a friendly conversation, you can say nothing and walk away. If the police say, "MOVE!" or give some other order, you may ask, "Why?" but you are advised not to say anything more. Notify a Legal Observer about the order. If the police ask to search you or your bag, you should say, "NO, I do not consent to a search." If the police search anyway, you are advised to continue to say, "I do not consent to a search." If you physically interfere with the search, you risk arrest. If the police question you, including asking your name, you may say nothing and walk away. If the police prevent you from leaving, ask, "Am I free to go?" If they answer "YES," you may say nothing and walk away. If they answer "NO," say, "I wish to remain silent. I want to talk to a lawyer," and wait for the police to arrest or release you.

"What can I do to prepare for a possible arrest?"

Write the Guild's phone number on your wrist or ankle; call this if you are arrested or if you see an arrest. Carry in your pocket several quarters to make telephone calls and a phone card for possible long distance calls. Carry a granola bar in your pocket; food is often missed in jail. Carry in your pocket one photo ID with a good address; do not carry ID with different addresses. Do not carry anything you do not want the police to have such as phone books or valuables.

"What do I do if I get arrested?"

You are advised to state clearly, "I am going to remain silent. I want to speak to a lawyer." Repeat this to any officer who questions you. Do not believe everything the police say—it is legal for the police to lie to you to get you to talk. When asked, you can give your name and address, show photo ID, and allow yourself to be photographed and fingerprinted for purposes of confirming ID; refusal to provide ID information will delay your release from jail. Remember your arresting officer's name and badge number. If you get to a phone, call the NLG and give names of other arrestees. Remain calm and prepare yourself for a possible wait in jail for 24–36 hours.

"What will happen to me if I am arrested?"

You will be handcuffed and driven to a jail or detention center and later taken to court. In the police's discretion, you may be released from jail with a summons or desk appearance ticket ("DAT"), which tells you when to return to court. If you are charged with a misdemeanor or felony, you will more likely "go through the system" to be arraigned before a judge—this means you will be in jail for 24 to 36 hours. Don't talk to anyone but a lawyer about the facts of your arrest. A court employee will interview you about community ties (address, employment, family) to help the judge determine whether to set bail or release you on your own recognizance ("ROR"); it's OK to answer these questions—just don't talk about your arrest. A lawyer will briefly meet you about your case. Get the lawyer's name and phone number. You will be arraigned on the charges against you before a judge. Your lawyer will enter your pleas; when in doubt, plead, "Not Guilty." Conditions for release are set, either bail money or ROR. The next court date is scheduled on a court slip for you to keep. You may be offered an Adjournment in Contemplation of Dismissal ("ACD"). If you agree, your case is adjourned for 6 months. If you are not arrested during the 6 months, the charge is dismissed and the case is sealed. If you are arrested during the 6 months, the case can be brought back to court. If this happens, you still have all the rights you would normally have with a criminal case, including the right to trial. An ACD is NOT a plea of "Guilty."

"What do I do if the police knock at my door?"

If anyone knocks, don't open the door. Ask "Who are you?" If it is the police ask, "What do you want?"

"We just want to talk to you." If they say they want to come in or talk with you, state: "I have nothing to say. Slide your business card under the door. My lawyer will call you." Move away from the door and call the NLG.

"We have a search warrant." You reply: "If you have a warrant, slip it under the door." If they do, read it to confirm it is the correct address; if it is, open the door, step back, and state "I am going to remain silent. I want to speak to a lawyer." A

warrant is sometimes limited to a specific room; make mental notes of where the police search. If they don't have a warrant, again reply, "I have nothing to say. Slide your business card under the door."

"We have an arrest warrant." You reply: "If you have a warrant, slip it under the door." If they do, read it to determine if it is a warrant for your arrest or for someone else. If it is for you [or someone inside], tell them you are coming out, step out and close and lock the door behind you and state "I am going to remain silent. I want to speak to a lawyer." Do not say or do anything else. If the arrest warrant is for someone not inside your home, state the person is not there (or does not live there) and ask for the police to slip a business card under the door. Do not say or do anything else.

"What if I am not a U.S. citizen?"

There are far greater risks involved if you are arrested and you are not a U.S. citizen. Talk to a lawyer before coming to a protest. Always carry the name and telephone number of an immigration lawyer. Carry any immigration papers you might have such as your "green card," I-94, or work authorization with you as well.

NLG Occupy legal hotlines
are available 24/7

New York City:	(212) 679-6018
Chicago:	(773) 309-1198
Bay Area:	(415) 285-1011
Miami:	(786) 548-0911
Philadelphia:	(267) 702-0477
Los Angeles:	(323) 696-2299
Washington, DC:	(202) 957 2445
New Orleans:	(504) 875-0019
Baltimore:	(410) 205-2850
Buffalo:	(716) 332-4658
Minnesota:	(612) 656-9108
Michigan:	(313) 963-0843
Portland:	(503) 902-5340
Boston:	(617) 227-7335
Bethlehem:	(267) 702-0477
Allentown, PA:	(267) 702-0477
Delaware:	(267) 702-0477
Harrisburg, PA:	(267) 702-0477
Houston, TX:	(713) 526-1515
Idaho:	(208) 991-4324

National Lawyers Guild
http://www.nlg.org

NOAM CHOMSKY

OCCUPY

OCCUPIED MEDIA
PAMPHLET SERIES

R. Black's cover art for the original edition
edition of *Occupy* by Noam Chomsky.

ABOUT THE AUTHOR

Noam Chomsky is known throughout the world for his groundbreaking work in linguistics and his relentless advocacy for democracy, freedom and self-determination. Author of dozens of books, among his most recent are *Power Systems: Conversations on Global Democratic Uprisings and the New Challenges to U.S. Empire* and *Making the the Future: Occupations, Interventions, Empire and Resistance.*

In 1988, Chomsky received the Kyoto Prize in Basic Science, given "to honor those who have contributed significantly to the scientific, cultural, and spiritual development of mankind." The prize noted that "Dr. Chomsky's theoretical system remains an outstanding monument of twentieth century science and thought. He can certainly be said to be one of the great academicians and scientists of this century."

Chomsky has supported the initiatives of the Occupy movement from its first weeks.

He lives in Lexington, Massachusetts.